£ 95

The Poetry of the Scots

Also by Duncan Glen

Hugh MacDiarmid and the Scottish Renaissance
In Appearances: Poems
The Individual and the Twentieth-Century Scottish Literary Tradition
Selected Essays of Hugh MacDiarmid (editor)
Whither Scotland? (editor)
Hugh MacDiarmid: A Critical Survey (editor)
Realities Poems
Akros Poetry 1965–82 (editor)
The Autobiography of a Poet
European Poetry in Scotland (edited with Peter France)
Makars' Walk
Twenty of the Best (editor)

The Poetry of the Scots

An Introduction
and Bibliographical Guide
to Poetry in
Gaelic, Scots, Latin
and English

Duncan Glen

EDINBURGH UNIVERSITY PRESS

© Duncan Glen 1991

Edinburgh University Press
22 George Square, Edinburgh

Typeset in 10/11½pt Palatino by Alden Multimedia and
printed by Hartnolls Limited, Bodmin, Cornwall.

British Library Cataloguing
in Publication Data
Glen, Duncan
  The poetry of the Scots.
  I. Title
  821.009411

ISBN 0 7486 0297 6 (cased)

The publisher acknowledges subsidy from the Scottish Arts Council towards the publication
of this volume.

Contents

SECTION IV: *First Renaissance Poets (Sixteenth-Seventeenth Centuries)*

SECTION V: *Ballads*

SECTION VI: *Eighteenth-Century Poets*

SECTION VII: *Nineteenth-Century Poets*

SECTION VIII: *Twentieth-Century Poets*

Dedicated to Margaret

Acknowledgements

In the twentieth century the range of Scottish poetry is known as it never has been in previous centuries. It is a startling thought to remember that the poetry of Robert Henryson – arguably the greatest of Scottish poets – suffered centuries of neglect. Major poets have been restored to a wide readership but so also many lesser poets have been moved out of the shadows cast by greater ones. Lowland Scottish critics and readers have become more knowledgeable about Gaelic poetry. This new and extended interest in all aspects of Scottish poetry, as in all areas of Scottish culture and history, is an aspect of the revival of the idea of an independent Scottish culture that can absorb 'foreign' influences without being dominated by them. The work of twentieth-century creative writers has given credence to that revival but the work of several generations of scholarly editors of texts has been important, as has that of critics and historians of Scottish poetry. Without their work we would not have our present extended knowledge of the poetry of the Scots.

All of us who write on Scottish poetry owe a debt to the Scottish Text Society, to the Gaelic Texts Society and to the many publishers, large and small, who have not been bound by purely commercial considerations in publishing scholarly texts of the poets and critical studies of their writings. Obviously this is important to scholars; it is also important to all creative writers and to all concerned with a living Scottish culture. It is important too for the uncluttered joy of reading good and great poetry.

The debt that I owe to the scholarly writers to whom I refer above cannot be overstated; without their work this book could not have been written. I am also indebted to scholars who have spared time to advise me at various times as I have written this book: Dr Tom Hubbard of the Scottish Poetry Library, Professor R.D.S. Jack of Edinburgh University, Dr Alexander Law, and Mr Ian MacDonald of the Gaelic Books Council who advised me beyond the call of duty on Gaelic matters. Of course all errors and omissions are mine.

I am grateful to the staffs of the following libraries for generously-given assistance: the Scottish Library of Edinburgh Central

Public Library, the Library of Edinburgh University, the Mitchell Library, Glasgow, the National Library of Scotland and the Scottish Poetry Library.

As with all my books, I am grateful to my wife for shrewd advice and for help with copy-preparation and for undertaking the typing of the final version of this book.

Duncan Glen
Marchmont, Edinburgh
December 1990

Ground Rules for Bibliographical Entries

The ground rules laid down for the bibliographical entries are aimed to give an entry into Scottish poetry for both the general and the scholarly reader. For pre-twentieth-century poets the most complete and the most scholarly modern edition of their work is listed. Other important modern editions are also listed and within the text reference is made to earlier editions which are still worthy of consultation. Where possible a 'Selected Poems' volume is listed; sometimes more than one such selection. The poets who are given a separate listing comprise all important poets; many lesser poets not so separately listed are referred to in the text. Anonymous work is given equal attention under various headings and is listed in the Index.

For the twentieth-century poets 'Complete Poems' or 'Collected Poems' editions are listed, as are 'Selected Poems' editions where such exist. For living poets with such 'Collected Poems' editions important works of poetry published after these major volumes are listed. For living poets who do not have a 'Collected Poems' edition a 'Selected Poems' edition is given, again followed by important collections published after the 'Selected Poems' volume. For living poets who have neither a 'Collected Poems' nor a 'Selected Poems' edition, all important collections of poetry are listed. Inevitably personal choice is involved in these listings, but they are made with regard to received opinion – that, of course, being influenced by currently acceptable critical opinions that later generations may reject. For the listing within Section VIII of 'C Twentieth-Century Renaissance Poets – Second and Third Waves' there is the lack of the critical judgments that only the perspective of later generations can have.

Following the listing of volumes of poetry by individual poets, details of critical books and important essays in periodicals are given. Volumes with essays on more than one poet are listed in 'Section I: Background Studies'. It is intended that quotations within the text from these, as from the other listed works, will not only extend my own knowledge and opinions but also refer interested readers to such works. The aim also is to indicate volumes that have bibliographies that extend into specialisations not listed here. This includes works such as the two volumes of the anthology *Longer Scottish Poems* in addition to scholarly histories or critical surveys such as *Scottish Poetry: A Critical Survey*, edited by James Kinsley, and the recently-published *The History of Scottish Literature*, general editor Cairns Craig, the four volumes of which are of major importance. Important single-author works are referred to for a similar reason; I would particularly refer to *An Introduction to Gaelic Poetry* by Derick Thomson.

The aim is also to indicate anthologies where a range of important poems can be easily found. For this purpose I have selected: *The Oxford Book of Scottish Verse* edited by John MacQueen and Tom Scott; *Longer Scottish Poems, Volume I,* edited by Priscilla Bawcutt and Felicity Riddy, and *Longer Scottish Poems, Volume II,* edited by Thomas Crawford, David Hewitt and Alexander Law; *A Choice of Scottish Verse,* edited by R.D.S. Jack; and *Modern Scottish Poetry* (various editions), edited by Maurice Lindsay. Other anthologies which make available poems not in these anthologies are also listed.

All the poets given a numbered entry and all other Scottish poets referred to in the text are given in the Index of Poets. The General Index also lists these poets as many of those of this twentieth century are also editors and critics. The General Index also refers to all editors and authors of books and essays given a numbered entry. The titles of numbered entries are not indexed as reference to an author gives easy access to them.

The date limit on entries is 31st December 1990 but a very few books of later date have been listed where there was reliable advance notice from publishers at that time and which I have seen before final proof-reading.

Introduction

The work of the poets, named or anonymous, introduced here is of a long tradition that goes back through the centuries to a time when the peoples of the land mass now known as Scotland would not have acknowledged such a social or political entity. This account of the poetry of the Scots is inevitably a partial one but I have attempted to make it one that reveals a response to the opinions of the many critics who have written on Scottish poetry. I attempt to avoid both a personal account of the poetry of the Scots and the dullness of restating received opinion.

The text of commentary on the poetry is introductory, as is this Introduction, but the bibliographical listings aim to be of use to both the general and the scholarly reader.

It is never easy to define a literary tradition and that of Scottish poetry is no exception. So also is it difficult to relate a diversity of poets to the wider history of a country. I aim in this Introduction to provide a few guidelines to both the literary tradition and to the history of Scotland.

The very name Scots is heavy with varying usages. In twentieth-century Scotland the Celtic language of the Highlands and Western Islands is termed Gaelic; the languages of the Lowlands today are Scots and English – or a mixture of the two which in varying language cocktails is the everyday speech and the literary language of most Lowland Scots and of some poets. The earliest Scottish Gaelic poetry has its roots in the classical Gaelic poetry of Ireland; the people from whom modern Scotland takes its name came from Ireland. In formal documents of medieval Scotland the Latin name for Scottish Gaelic was *lingua Scotica*, being the language of the aforesaid 'Scots'. By the fifteenth century the Lowland term for Gaelic was *Erse* or Irish; the language that had become the medium for major poets of the Lowlands was termed *Inglis*. This term was used to distinguish it from the language of Southern England which can be termed *English*. The first Lowland poet to call his language *Scottis* was Gavin Douglas in his first Prologue to his translation of Virgil's *Aeneid* which he completed in 1513. A little later, however, the poet Sir David Lyndsay referred to his language as *Inglis*.

That these medieval Lowland Scottish poets and official documents of the time referred to this language as *Inglis* reveals the antecedents of Scots. It was introduced into what is now termed Scotland by Anglian settlers from Northumbria; these people were descendants of the Saxons as well as of the Angles from whom modern England takes its name. These settlers, or conquerors, were well established by the seventh century. Aneirin's great poem, *The Gododdin*, which is written in a very early form of what is now Welsh, tells uniquely of a losing battle fought by the Celts against these Angles; Aneirin tells a story of men of flesh and blood who still live in his great heroic poem.

In 1066, to leap ahead and compress this complicated history of Scotland's languages, came the Norman conquest of England. The defeated royal Saxons came north and one consequence of this was the further anglicisation of Scotland. Margaret of the royal house of Essex became queen of the widowed Malcolm III, King of Scots, and she and her sons were the instigators of this anglicisation and movement away from the old Celtic Scotland. With Malcolm begins the Canmore dynasty and they were to rule Scotland for more than two hundred years. Margaret was canonised and the chapel of Saint Margaret is today the oldest building in Edinburgh Castle. The Normans came to Scotland also, as great names in Scottish history reveal – Bruce, Comyn and Balliol – and they spoke French. King Robert Bruce, King of Scots, however spoke Gaelic and French and the victor of the Battle of Bannockburn in 1314 which assured Scottish independence from England reveals in his knowledge of Gaelic the extent of that language up to that date; even in the sixteenth century half of the population of Scotland spoke Gaelic.

The first Stewart king, Robert II, came to the Scottish throne in 1371. King Robert Bruce's daughter, Marjorie Bruce, married Walter Stewart, the Beardless, less than a year after the victory at Bannockburn. Their son, born in March 1316 after his mother had been thrown from her horse, as a result of which she died, was Robert II. The only Stewart to speak Gaelic was James IV and he was an exceptional linguist fluent in many languages. At the court of the Stewarts French could be spoken and the language of learning was Latin. In the Lowlands the future lay with *Inglis*, which I will now term Scots, infused by French forms from the Norman influence. In the fourteenth century this was already the language of major Lowland Scottish poetry; this is the time of Middle Scots, the language of Barbour being Early Scots.

Poetry in Scots has been influenced by English work, and that of Chaucer was significant in the great poetry of Robert Henryson in the fifteenth century, but this in no way justifies the once-common description of him as one of the Scottish Chaucerians – already this is a poetry of an independent Scots tradition. In the work of Gavin Douglas are to be found perhaps more English forms than in Henryson, but the translator of Virgil's *Aeneid* also extended the range of his vernacular language by introducing French and Latin forms. He, like Henryson, reveals humanistic influences. After the union of the Scottish and English crowns in 1603 and the removal of the Scottish court to London, English became one of the languages of Scottish poetry and it became even more important with the union of the Scottish and English parliaments in 1707, although the eighteenth century also saw a revival of poetry in Scots. In this eighteenth-century work, including that of Robert Burns, there is often a mixing of Scots and English forms. This is still an important aspect of Scottish poetry today, alongside the work written in Scottish-English and in Gaelic which remains remarkably free of English or Scots forms.

I would refer interested readers initially to *Languages of Scotland* edited by A.J. Aitken and Tom McArthur and for French influences on medieval Scots poetry to Janet M. Smith's *The French Background of Middle Scots Literature.* The Italian influence is less important with regard to the Middle Scots poets but it became more important later and this has been admirably revealed by R.D.S. Jack in his *The Italian Influence on Scottish Literature* and *Scottish Literature's Debt to Italy.*

The senior language of Scotland, as I have indicated above, is Gaelic. For many centuries the classical Gaelic tradition which developed from that of Ireland was the major literature of what is now Scotland. It was a poetry of scholarship and learning and was highly structured in its forms and metres. The poets of this classical Gaelic poetry learned the disciplines and these traditional forms in the bardic schools. The bardic poets had an important place in medieval Scotland at the courts of the Gaelic chiefs and formed hereditary lines, as did the bards of Ireland. Indeed, the important line of the MacMhuirichs was founded by Muireadhach Albanach Ó Dálaigh, an Irish poet who had fled to Scotland as a consequence of some murderous act. The MacMhuirichs provided official poets to the Lords of the Isles, who will reappear in this Introduction, and later to the Clanranald branch of the Clan Donald – this perhaps extending to eighteen generations by the eighteenth century. To listen to a roll-call of these bards is to hear not only an aspect of Scottish history but also a catalogue worthy of any bard – or of Ovid himself – although a classical Gaelic bard might not regard that as a relevant comparison or as a compliment.

In his *An Introduction to Gaelic Poetry* Derick Thomson gives statistics of the work of the bardic poetry that has come down to us. To condense his analysis, there are some 160 items; the bulk of these belong to the period 1450–1650 and little work of the post-1700 period has survived. What has survived is very often a matter of chance and may not indicate the range of the work of the bards at any given time.

An important source for this Scottish bardic poetry is *The Book of the Dean of Lismore*. These 'official' or professional bards wrote as the occasion demanded and the Dean's collection reveals a wide range of subject-matter. The 'routine' work of the bards, however, was as chroniclers of genealogy and history; this being in the context of the 'praise poem' which often merged chronicle and lyric. The bards were also the 'Government' or 'Party' information officers of their day and, as has been apparent in the 1980s, such men can be very powerful.

The 'Classical Early Modern' period of Scottish Gaelic literature, with its Irish links, lasted from, say, the twelfth to the seventeenth century. If it began with the powerful Lordship of the Isles and a Gaelic-speaking aristocracy, it declined as the patronage of these chiefs was withdrawn in the Covenanting and Jacobite times of the seventeenth and eighteenth centuries. I would refer interested readers initially to W. Gillies's essay, 'Gaelic: The Classical Tradition', in *The History of Scottish Literature, Volume I*.

The vernacular tradition in Gaelic verse has been influenced by the classical one but these vernacular poets belong essentially in a different world of poetry from that of the learned poets. This is not to suggest that the vernacular is necessarily a lesser poetry, and many modern readers find it more accessible. In the seventeenth century the satirical poetry of Iain Lom (John MacDonald) was very much a poetry of the clans in subject-matter but it remains relevant to us today and not least so for the cutting edge of his spare but powerful language. His earliest work belonged to the 1640s and his last poem known to us is a magnificent example of bawdy invective written in 1707. This poet of scathing satire was then in his eighties and he lambasted the bribe-takers of the Lowlands whom he saw as having sold out to the English in engineering the union of the Scottish and English parliaments. To this seventeenth century belong also the songs of Mary MacLeod, but these could have co-existed with the work of the learned bards at the courts of the chiefs as Gaelic society has always been enriched by song and song-makers. The heroic ballads and heroic-romantic tales also co-existed with the learned classical poetry. The genuine lays of the heroic ballad tradition lie behind the Ossianic creations of James Macpherson in the eighteenth century. Macpherson's work may have been fake, but through it the Celtic culture of Ireland and Scotland was a powerful influence on non-Celtic European poetry. For an authoritative critical history of Gaelic poetry I would refer readers to Derick Thomson's *An Introduction to Gaelic Poetry*.

If it is difficult to define a national tradition in poetry, it is impossible to separate the Lowland Scottish one from the wider European one. John Barbour is sometimes referred to as 'the father of Scottish poetry' but that is to ignore the many good poets who must have gone before him. He is, however, the first major poet whose work has survived. His epic of the Wars of Independence, *Bruce*, shows the influence of what fragments of earlier Scots work we know but it is also of a wider European tradition in which French models predominate. The Scottish poet accepts the conventions of the French tradition in epic poetry with regard to its forms and its attitude to the subject-matter, but makes it uniquely Scottish. Barbour probably wrote his *Bruce* between 1375 and 1377 but as his aim was to tell it as it was – history remade as poetry – long research may have preceded these years of writing.

John Barbour may have been encouraged in his work by Robert II who came to the throne in February 1371 aged almost fifty-five; he died in 1390. This was a vicious time in Scottish history as in European, if any time can be said to be more so than another. In these medieval days the battle for power was between kings and barons. In the Highlands the chiefs of the Clan Donald to whom the MacMhuirich Gaelic bards owed their position – and power and lands – assumed the title of Lord of the Isles about 1354. Of the Stewarts, only James VI succeeded even partially in imposing the will of central government upon the Highland chiefs who were as powerful as, and, despite the Celtic clan structure, not so very different in fundamentals from the famous, or infamous, Black Douglases in the south. The power of these Douglases came from Lord James Douglas ('Good Sir James') who was one of Bruce's principal lieutenants at Bannockburn. The Black Douglases as Earls of Douglas retained great power for centuries, as did the Red Douglases as Earls of Angus. A man of the Red Douglas family is Gavin Douglas the poet, and the intertwining of the power of the great and powerful families of Scotland emerges in any introduction to the lives of Scottish poets. Mostly the patronage enjoyed by the poets came, however, from the kings rather than the nobility, and until 1603 much of Lowland Scottish poetry was a poetry of the Stewart court. Alongside that courtly poetry, however, there was always a strand of popular poetry, often of a comic nature.

Robert II was succeeded by Robert III who certainly did not effectively challenge the power of the barons, perhaps having been debilitated by being kicked by a horse. His words for his own epitaph were, 'Here lies the worst of kings and the most wretched of men in the whole realm'. In these words is the essence of the tragedy of a man who was too good for the times he lived in. He was succeeded in 1406 by his son James I who, aged only eleven, was the first of a succession of child kings and one child queen.

The boy was captured at sea by the English, perhaps in a time of truce, only a month before he became king, and spent eighteen years in captivity in England. The violence continued in Scotland in his absence and on his return that world of violence was his world. Yet he is the first poet of sophistication who wrote in Scots and whose work has come down to us. *The Kingis Quair* is very much of the tradition of French courtly poetry growing out of the poetry of *amour courtois*, but James extended that poetry of love and, in Ezra Pound's excellent phrase, 'made it new'. The poem's language shows the influence of the poet's years in England, but this use of both English and Scots forms was to continue throughout the centuries and continues to this day. This has been regretted by nationalistic critics, but for Scots poetry to absorb the English forms is surely no weakening of the Scots tradition as long as the native tradition is extended by the absorption of these foreign elements and not overwhelmed by them. The medieval Scots-writing poets certainly benefited from the eclecticism of their language. So also, I would suggest, did Robert Burns in the eighteenth century in some of his major poems, as did Hugh MacDiarmid in this twentieth century. This infusion of 'foreign' elements may, indeed, be one of the characteristics of Scots poetry.

That James I was the author of *The Kingis Quair* has been questioned and therefore also that the poem is based on autobiography. The young king was released from captivity in 1424, soon after his marriage to Lady Joan Beaufort in February of that year. In this complex and beautiful poem the speech of Minerva reveals fulfilment in a marriage of love. The date of the poem has also aroused much interesting scholarly debate; I find the date of 1435 pleasing in relation to the date of the king's marriage and to his continuing happiness in it as revealed in the poem. The conclusion reached in the poem is of the right to have confidence in a future based on a philosophy of love that is based on marriage. Only two years after 1435 the poet-king was dead — brutally murdered in the Blackfriars convent at Perth on the night of 20/21 February 1437.

The Kingis Quair is highly sophisticated court poetry, but alongside it should be put a strong vein of popular poetry that runs through the Scots tradition. The comic 'Colkelbie Sow' is an excellent example of this wild tradition and the very influential 'Chrystis Kirk on the Grene' is a poem of rustic conviviality, being of what has been termed the 'peasant brawl' tradition in Scots poetry. It may be, however, that James I was the author of this poem, poets being capable of many a persona.

Sir Richard Holland's *The Buke of the Howlat*, which was written perhaps some ten years after the death of James I, is of the alliterative tradition which remained important in Scotland after it had ceased to be so in England. Holland's poem is in the thirteen-line stanza form which was also used by the anonymous author of the comic masterpiece *The Taill of Rauf Coilyear* which, as Felicity Riddy has shrewdly suggested, is a work that is best read as a 'literary game or a playful spoof'. Gavin Douglas uses the same alliterative form in his satirising of the alliterative dream-vision tradition in the eighth Prologue to his translation of Virgil's *Aeneid*; Douglas's Prologue comes almost seventy years after Holland wrote his *Howlat* poem.

These poems involving the demands of both alliteration and rhyme – the beginnings and the endings of words – reveal the linguistic range of poetry in Scots of this time. Later poetry may be more obviously sophisticated but it does not exceed this in metrical skills or in vigour. One of the strengths of poetry in Scots has always been the sheer physical qualities inherent in the language. William Dunbar's great 'The Tretis of the Twa Mariit Wemen and the Wedow' reveals this almost beyond comparison and the *Tretis* is of this same alliterative tradition as Holland's poem although the long lines of Dunbar's poem are unrhymed, which is unusual in the Scots alliterative work that we know. Towards the end of the sixteenth century James VI was to see the triple rhythms of alliterative verse as the metre of flyting, or cumulative abuse and insults, but the tradition has been important beyond that indicated by James.

Sir Richard Holland benefited from the patronage of Elizabeth Dunbar, who became a countess as the wife of the Earl of Moray, one of the powerful Douglas family. Holland was in the household of the Earl in the north of Scotland and indeed his poem of the *Howlat* is set in the grounds of the castle of the earl and countess at Darnaway in Morayshire. A humanist such as Gavin Douglas may have regarded, at least for the purposes of his satirical eighth Prologue, the vernacular alliterative tradition as parochial, but Holland's poem is, in its variety of styles and levels of language, a most sophisticated work of art by a makar confident in the varying traditions within which he worked. Also, Holland, quite as much as Gavin Douglas, accepted quite naturally the idea of a Europe with interlocking cultures despite the warfare between nations. To Holland, a Council of Nations would quite naturally have had the King of Scots as a member.

It may be that a greater poet – perhaps Scotland's greatest – Robert Henryson – was writing his finest poems about the time of Holland's death in the 1480s and if this is so it could be said that his is the greatest European poetry of these years. Assuming this dating to be correct, and that Henryson was dead by 1490, his poetry belongs to the reign of James III who came to the throne at the age of eight in August 1460 when James II was killed by the bursting of one of his own cannons whilst besieging Roxburgh Castle, having been 'mair curios nor becam him or the majestie of ane king'. So do writers put kings into perspective. In these times of war and pillage the young King James III is said to have hated war, but of course he was forced into it although his real interests were in civilised pursuits. One attempt to encourage music-making antagonised the powerful baronial family of the Humes by asking Pope

Innocent VIII to suppress Coldingham Priory and assign half of its revenues to the Chapel Royal. The king had the admirable intention of developing the Chapel as a music school. The Humes had previously received the revenues and they did not take kindly to the king's action – and, in their turn, took violent action which led to James III's death. His end is comic-tragic and violent. Leaving the field of a battle near Stirling, his horse bolted and threw him; he was taken to a cottage at Beaton's Mill near Bannockburn and there he was murdered; the date was 11th June 1488.

This is a world seemingly far removed from that of the poet Henryson, who may have been both lawyer and schoolmaster in Dunfermline, Fife, but although the other medieval world of Henryson is as far removed from us today as that of kings and barons in its view of the world in social, philosophical or scientific terms, his civilising poetry remains as relevant to the human condition as when it was written in these savage days.

To the troubled reign of James III belongs also a very different poetry but in its own way an equally important one, and a truly original work for the Europe of its time. I refer to Hary's epic *Wallace* which was perhaps written between 1476 and 1478. Superior critics have under-estimated Hary's achievement, seeing him as a somewhat uncouth Barbour. This, however, is a work that has moved the imaginations of centuries of Scots. It is a truly heroic tale of Sir William Wallace, the great freedom fighter and leader of the resistance movement that fought against the dominance of Scotland by England in the last years of the thirteenth century. As a dramatic tale it has a conclusion that equals any in heroic epic or romance – the execution of Wallace in London in August 1305. Every Scot has relived the injustice of the barbarous death of Wallace. Hary's epic powerfully reveals a human hatred of the English that is lacking in the more detached epic that is Barbour's *Bruce*, written a hundred years earlier. But Hary's *Wallace* is a universal epic that could move William Wordsworth as it moved Robert Burns. It is a poem of achieved form that has only recently been recognised for the high-art form that it is. The poetry of Henryson and Hary alone makes the reign of James III as important for poetry as that of his more celebrated successor, James IV.

If James III was a king who avoided publicity, James IV was quite the reverse. He was fifteen years old when his father was assassinated. His reign has been seen as the golden age of medieval Scotland, and not least so with regard to poetry. This is the high point of Scottish court poetry; the age of William Dunbar and Gavin Douglas. The former is the courtier poet *par excellence*, even if a not inconsiderable number of his poems is devoted to anger at his lack of advancement at court. Ranald Nicholson has termed this the 'aureate age' in Scottish history and certainly that applies to the language of both Dunbar and Douglas, although Henryson could write similarly when he thought it appropriate. James IV was an inspiring if impetuous leader with style and panache who wished his court to be celebrated throughout Europe, as were other richer and greater ones. This was as much about knightly tournaments as civilising Acts, but at court William Dunbar had his place, even if not as favoured a one as he sought, although his bitterness at his unfair treatment gives more than a little bite to some of his poems. Of quite a different kind are poems which are an aspect of the ceremonial nature of the court of James IV. At least three of his poems must have graced the festivities of the wedding of the King to his young bride, Margaret Tudor, daughter of Henry VII of England and sister of Henry VIII. The wedding took place on 8th August 1503. Dunbar's 'The Thrissill and the Rois' may have been written for the child bride's arrival at Holyrood the previous day and was certainly written before the wedding.

Gavin Douglas, although also a courtier, belonged to a quite different world from Dunbar, being of the powerful Red Douglas family. He was the third son of Archibald, fifth Earl of Angus, otherwise known as Bell-the-Cat, who acquired this nickname by taking the lead in a conspiracy against James III. The poet was born perhaps in 1475 and, to take two typical incidents, his larger-than-life father was five years later leading the army that burnt Bamburgh Castle, and two years after that was involved in the hanging of favourites of James III at Lauder village and in imprisoning the King in Edinburgh Castle. In the early years of James IV's reign he was in treasonable correspondence with the English and in this his youngest son Gavin was to follow his example. Bell-the-Cat was to die soon after Flodden and his two elder sons on the battlefield. His grandson, and nephew of the poet, who succeeded to the title, was to marry Margaret Tudor, widow of James IV, and if we follow the line far enough, and it is a direct one through James VI, we come to our present Queen.

It is said that Bell-the-Cat was illiterate, but his poet son was to write perhaps the most impressive range of language of any Scots writer; in other ways, however, he resembled his father, being as much involved in traitorous politics as he had been. The poet was at court during the minority of James V, indeed, 'all the court was rewlit by the Erle of Angus, Mr Gawin Dowglass, and the Drummonds – bot nocht weill'. These vile politics came after the great poetry; his greatest literary achievement, and one of the great works of Scottish literature, is his translation of Virgil's *Aeneid* which he completed in the summer of 1513. Only weeks later, on 9th September, the hero-king James IV was dead on Flodden Field; all over Scotland was heard the 'lilt of dule and wae'.

Much has been written of that day in 1513, presented as that on which the great age of Scots poetry came to an end. But traditions in poetry are not as responsive to the death of a king and half of the nobility of a nation as that would suggest. The poetry that was written in the following century may not be the equal of that by Henryson, Dunbar and Douglas, but it is important.

The poetry of Sir David Lyndsay belongs to the reign of James V and part of the subsequent regency, say between 1528 and 1552. In Lyndsay we again have a courtier poet. He was a Master Usher to James V from the King's birth but when the Queen Mother and her husband, the sixth Earl of Angus, nephew of Gavin Douglas, came to power Lyndsay lost his minor offices; however, he was back in favour when in the spring of 1528 James V escaped from his keeper and the sixth Earl of Angus had to flee to England. The poet became Lord Lyon, King-of-Arms, and remained in favour until the King's death.

Lyndsay was a satirist of the highest level, if of a lower order as a poet. He was of the Protestant side in his satirising of the Catholic clergy, but to see his poetry in such simplistic terms is to under-estimate it — he is the intellectual asking questions of a wider range than those concerning only theology. His attacks on the Old Church helped to create a climate of opinion on moral as well as theological attitudes that enabled the Reformation to take Scotland into new political and economic attitudes and structures. In addition, by introducing an English translation of the Bible into every Lowland Scottish home, the Reformers gave the English language a status in Scotland which it had never previously enjoyed.

James V seems to have accepted Lyndsay's satirical work with surprising benevolence, despite its encompassing the idea of serving leadership, an attitude which had been seen, uniquely for that time, in Barbour's *Bruce*. This attitude is revealed again in Lyndsay's poetry and is perhaps exemplified by the words, 'Quhat is a king bot ane officer'. It has been said that James V was 'the poor man's king' and, although no doubt for reasons of power and politics, the Stewart kings did tend to be kings of the people rather than of the nobles. This is the voice of Scotland that is heard in the poetry of Scotland and which is a stubborn 'democratic' base in the history of the Scots despite all the power of a few noble families. So also is it a characteristic of the Scots tradition in poetry.

The idea of James V as the 'gaberlunzie king' who went about incognito amongst his people made him in my childhood, and perhaps still today, a favourite with Scottish schoolchildren. In later life I was told by the worldly-wise that this was a lecherous king seeking village lasses, although he did not lack opportunities in more courtly circles. Recent historians have dealt harshly with James V; Gordon Donaldson, for example, writing, 'Perhaps James is not to be judged by Scottish standards. He was, after all, half a Tudor by birth and perhaps a Tudor rather than a Stewart in character. He combined in his own person the acquisitiveness of his grandfather, Henry VII, the lust and ruthlessness of his uncle, Henry VIII, and the unrelenting cruelty of his cousin, Bloody Mary.' The paradoxes of James V's life will never be resolved, any more than those of the Scots literary tradition with its delight in the formal, offset by a passion for the seemingly uncontrolled; or again what I have referred to above as its 'democratic base' offset by a desire for authoritarianly-imposed discipline. This is to be seen in the post-Reformation stance of the individual Scot speaking to his God face to face but within the disciplines – the law and logic – of Calvinism.

The story of James V's death in Falkland Palace was also part of my junior school education, but it was only in later years that I appreciated the personal sadness of the King's death; the tragedy of the deaths of his two sons and the humiliating disaster of the battle at Solway Moss on 24th November 1542. After the battle the will to live seems to have gone from the King, although he was only thirty years of age. His spirit broken, he turned his face to the wall with, according to his favourite poet, David Lyndsay, a 'litill smyle of lauchtir' and with the famous last words told to us in class, 'It cam wi a lass and it'll gang wi a lass'.

The first lass was Marjorie Bruce, daughter of Robert Bruce, King of Scots, victor of Bannockburn; the second lass was to be Mary, Queen of Scots. Just days before he turned his face to the wall the King had received word of Mary's birth at Linlithgow. Not for the first time in the history of the Stewart monarchs a child was on the throne of Scotland, if never before such a young infant as Mary. The child-queen's nearest male kinsman was her great-uncle, King Henry VIII of England, who had been blessed with a son now of suitable age to marry the little Queen of Scots. As always with rulers of England, Henry's aim was to set up circumstances which would result in England taking over the Kingdom of Scotland. Before long it was agreed in the treaties of Greenwich that Mary would be married to the English Prince Edward. Not for the first time, nor for the last, a ruler of England behaved presumptuously to the Kingdom of Scotland, but was snubbed. The English prince was rejected and on 7th July 1548 a treaty was made with the French that Mary should marry the Dauphin. A month later the five-year-old Queen was safely in France to be educated alongside the French monarch's children.

It may be that among the entourage that accompanied the young Queen Mary to France was the poet Alexander Scott. This is not to suggest that Scott was a courtier in the sense that Dunbar or the differently-placed Gavin Douglas had been. If Scott went with the Queen it was as a companion of Maister John Erskine, who was Prior of Inchmahome and was later to be, as Earl of Mar, a regent during James VI's childhood. One of the few poems by Alexander Scott that has survived that is not a love poem is 'Lament of the Maister of Erskine'. The future Earl of Mar was the younger brother of the subject of this poem. The poet seems to have been an organist at Inchmahome Priory and if this is so we can perhaps assume that he was appointed to that post, being a Canon, as a result of his commemorative poem on the future Mar's elder brother. It is perhaps further relevant to note that Mar was succeeded in 1572 as regent in James VI's childhood by the much more powerful James Douglas, fourth Earl of Morton, who was a nephew of the sixth Earl of Angus, nephew of Gavin Douglas. I give this convoluted account of inter-relationships to reveal the small world that was Scotland in the sixteenth century – not that much has changed today.

Before he was at Inchmahome Priory, according to John MacQueen, Alexander Scott seems to have been attached to the Chapel Royal at Stirling as a musician, perhaps in the late 1530s. I give these details to indicate the world in which Scott lived but also to emphasise the fact that he was a musician, composer and arranger. His lyrical poetry was written for music but, as Maurice Lindsay has suggested, he wrote his songs for part-song rather than, as Robert Burns did, for monodic folk-air. The similarity with Burns can be seen not only in their great poems that are also songs, but also in their love poetry, which is among the finest in the Scots language.

Of the thirty-six poems by Scott that have survived – or survived under his name – only two, excepting his versions of two Psalms, are not about love. The metrical range of his work is a joy, as is the complexity of his portrayal of the many variables that comprise the human 'game' of love; as with many poets, the game of poetry and life are as one. Mary, Queen of Scots, returned to Scotland, landing at Leith on 16th August 1561, and one of the two poems referred to above is 'Ane New Yeir Gift to the Quene Mary, quhen scho come first Hame: 1562'.

The biography of Alexander Scott has aroused as much interesting scholarly debate as, for example, the dating of James I's (assuming that he is the author) *The Kingis Quair* but I find John MacQueen's propositions on the life of Scott pleasing, as I do these of those who indicate an autobiographical base to *The Kingis Quair* and the dating of it as 1435. I would refer interested readers to Professor MacQueen's essay on Scott's biography in *Scotland and the Lowland Tongue*, edited by J. Derrick McClure.

When Mary Queen of Scots left France Pierre de Ronsard was to write a poem of sad melancholy on the event and in Scotland the poet Sir Richard Maitland of Lethingtoun warmly welcomed her return. Maitland continued the long line of Scottish courtier poets as he was at the court of James V and remained a faithful servant to the King's widow and to Mary on her return to Scotland. He did not, however, turn poet till his old age although it was a long one as he lived until ninety, and some of his best poems were written from the viewpoint of an old man. Although Maitland was too old to have power during Mary's reign, his eldest son, William, was Secretary to Mary and was involved in the often treacherous intrigues that surrounded her. His second son, John, was to become James VI's Chancellor and the first in that century who was neither prelate nor peer; he became Lord Thirlestane. Both wrote poetry and again we have the contradiction of ruthless men in the power game of politics being at the same time men of civilised poetry. Sir Richard Maitland lived to see the young James VI emerge as a powerful personality of considerable political ability. He was also another poet-king, if a lesser one than James I.

Also at Mary's court was George Buchanan, the greatest Scottish Latinist. He had high hopes of the young queen as he revealed most gloriously in his verse dedication to her at the head of his translations of the Psalms. Later Buchanan became tutor to James VI when the King was only four years old and, bullying him unmercifully, did nothing to ease his pupil's tortured childhood. When James VI became a leader of poets whom he thought could write a distinctively Scottish poetry, he wrote, 'They gar me speik Latin ar I could speik Scottis'. Perhaps like many another he was reacting against an authoritarian teacher.

The king who later ruled both Scotland and England may have been a creature of devious political contortions, although not the comic figure portrayed in Walter Scott's *The Fortunes of Nigel*, but he survived what must have been the hell of his childhood remarkably well. Equally remarkably, the young king when not yet twelve years of age began to assert himself on this bloody stage from which he must have known he could be summarily removed at any time.

The Svengali behind the boy-king was his relative, Esmé Stewart, seigneur D'Aubigny, who had arrived from France in September 1579 and was soon to be Earl of Lennox and a year later, in 1581, Duke of Lennox. This was a time of conflict between Catholics and Protestants and Esmé Stewart was powerful and successful in the vicious politics of the day, succeeding in having the powerful Douglas, Earl of Morton, beheaded by the 'Maiden', which was a variation of the guillotine introduced into Scotland by its victim in the days of his power. For a literary man's view of the prose writings of these times, see Maurice Lindsay's *History of Scottish Literature*. A man of interesting name on the Catholic side who debated as fiercely as Knox did with his Queen was Ninian Winzet, and Dr Lindsay also gives a picture of a deviously political George Buchanan that varies from the equally accurate view of him as a civilised and distinguished Latinist. By 1587 that master politician James VI was already thinking of himself as a possible heir to the throne of England − always his main ambition − and was negotiating with

Elizabeth. The rights and wrongs of his defence of his mother are not my concern here, but Buchanan had tried to indoctrinate the young man into believing that his mother was involved in his father's murder. This again I detail to reveal the times in which that young man lived. On 8th February 1587 Mary was beheaded at Fotheringay.

The influence of Esmé Stewart on the young James VI extended beyond the vicious politics of that cruel age as he came to the Scottish court knowledgable about French literature. Perhaps influenced also by the poet Alexander Montgomerie, the King began to write poetry. He also became a theorist of poetry, a critic who advocated new directions for Scottish poetry. His aim was no less than to restore poetry in Scots to the creative heights of the auld makars of the time of James III and James IV when Henryson and Dunbar wrote their great poetry. The critic-king wished, however, no facile imitation of these great poets. He looked to Europe for the fundamentals of his critical theories and followed the example of, amongst others, Du Bellay in reacting against over-strong humanist influences in poetry. The critic-king advocated a distinctively Scots vernacular poetry as Du Bellay had advocated a vernacular French one; in this, James was of his European time. The projection of a distinctively Scottish poetry is therefore in its nationalism not a provincial reaction but quite the reverse. The royal leader of a renaissance of poetry in Scots wished that poetry to continue to be acknowledged as of the European tradition. Towards achieving this James encouraged the poets he had gathered around him at court – his Castalian Band – to translate European poetry into Scots. The major achievement in translation was John Stewart of Baldynneis's shortened version of Ariosto's *Orlando Furioso* into vigorous Scots. Soon, however, James was to become also James I of England and to take his court south to London; the noble tradition of Stewart court poetry thus came to an end in 1603.

James VI's ambition for the poets of his court – for his Castalian Band – was that they should write a 'new' Scots poetry. The major poet of his renaissance – his 'maister poet' – however, was Alexander Montgomerie who had established himself as a major poet in Mary's reign. Montgomerie was a late example of a Scottish poet who was very much involved in major political events. His life was a veritable saga worthy of heroic poetry in the ballad tradition of both Highlands and Lowlands. That tale, of political intrigue worthy of Gavin Douglas and of daring deeds, I leave to others. As a poet Montgomerie is important as a maker of songs, but his major importance is as the author of the longer poem 'The Cherrie and the Slae' which he may have begun to write in 1584, around the time when James VI was beginning to act as a Scottish Maecenas. In essentials this is not a 'new' Scots poem such as James envisaged, rather it is a work that is rich with echoes of earlier Scots poetry. It is one of these major works in a literary tradition that brings together many strands of that tradition and yet is also something new. In the eighteenth century Burns similarly was to gather together the elements of a tradition and out of it create new and unique poems. I would further suggest that, for all James VI's ambition for a new poetry in Scots, it is probable that Montgomerie would have written very little differently from what he did if his king had never involved himself in forming his Castalian band of poets. James did, however, influence the lesser poets, including Stewart of Baldynneis into his translation of Ariosto. How Scottish poetry would have developed if James had not succeeded to the English throne is another question.

I would return to the reality of Montgomerie's 'The Cherrie and the Slae'. This is a major poem within the Scots tradition in poetry, once a 'bestseller' of its time. It is centrally of the Scots tradition but, as with all major Scots-writing poets, Montgomerie also drew upon the wider European tradition, as in the allegorical aspects of his masterpiece. The fourteen-line stanza with bob and wheel, as T.F. Henderson indicates in his *Scottish Vernacular Poetry: A History* (1898), is of a ten-line stave that was common in England from the early fourteenth century plus 'a peculiar wheel borrowed from a stave of the old Latin Hymns'. This form was used by Burns in the 'Recitativo' of his 'The Jolly Beggars'. It may be that Mongomerie's 'The Cherrie and the Slae' was written to be sung and, as Maurice Lindsay suggests, 'its intricacy dictated at least in part by the steps of a dance and its music'. I would refer interested readers to Helena Mennie Shire's *Song, Dance and Poetry at the Court of Scotland under James VI.*

The politics of these poets are those of the Reformation. Montgomerie was fully committed to the Catholic cause and intrigued and fought mightily for it and perhaps even died for it. A rather different poet active at James's court in the 1580s was Alexander Hume. He was firmly of the Protestant camp and his 'Of the Day Estivall' reveals the essential religious nature of all his poetry, but in this masterpiece there is not a hint of what is popularly regarded as the suppressive stance of men of the Reformation towards works of art, or towards a true acceptance of the joy in life. Certainly all is rejoicing in this poem of a heavenly day. If the conventionally-received view of the aspect of Scottish culture that is termed Calvinistic is sometimes a distorting one, the consensus view of a nature poetry being an important aspect of Scottish poetry is perhaps less so. Certainly Hume's poem belongs with the nature poetry that is in Henryson, Douglas and, after Hume, James Thomson, even if it is commonplace to say so. This aspect of Scottish poetry is also to be seen in the description of a summer morning in Montgomerie's 'The Cherrie and the Slae' which is another indication of the many essential characteristics of the Scots tradition to be found in this beautiful poem. I would refer interested readers to J. Veitch's *The Feeling for Nature in Scottish Poetry* (1887).

Many of James's Scottish poets accompanied him to London and attempted, as did the King, to be as Englishmen. If royal patronage or a supporting cultural climate conducive to the writing of a certain type of poetry could result in poets achieving major forms, we would have it in the days of James's Scottish court, and the reverse of that would be that removal of the court to London would have resulted in yet another blind coming down on Scottish poetry, as some have suggested happened after the disastrous Battle of Flodden. In fact a poet emerged after the court's removal who wrote more important poetry than any of James's Castalian Band, with the exception of Alexander Montgomerie. I refer to William Drummond of Hawthornden who remained in Scotland writing poetry far superior to anything produced by the Scottish poets who went south with James, such as Sir William Alexander who became Secretary of State in 1626, and Sir Robert Ayton who was secretary to both Queen Anne and Henrietta Maria. The interrelationships within this world of politics and poetry can be seen in the fact that William Fowler, who had been one of James's Castalian Band in Edinburgh and was secretary to Queen Anne, was Drummond's uncle.

William Drummond of Hawthornden is one of the most European of Scottish poets, his poetry being, if anything, over-rich in echoes of the love poetry of renaissance Europe. Also Drummond could be said to have broken all the rules of accepted criticism of the language question in relation to Scottish poetry by speaking Scots but writing in English, thus revealing himself as a follower of fashion and in nationalist terms a quisling to the independent Scottish literary tradition of the great Scots-writing poets. As always, a poet can prove wrong the theories of what should be his 'proper' language. Hugh MacDiarmid's defence of his language can be applied equally to Drummond who, in rejecting Scots and turning to English did the reverse of MacDiarmid who wrote in 1932, 'It cannot be too strongly emphasised that it is absurd to debate whether Scots affords as good a medium as any other language for literary purposes. Any language, real or artificial, serves if a creative artist finds his medium in it. In other words, it does not depend at all upon any other consideration, but wholly upon the *rara avis*, the creative artist himself.' The poets who went south with James VI failed to find a suitable medium in English; William Drummond, who remained in Scotland, did achieve through the medium of the English language a significant poetry. Of course it can be asked whether he would have achieved even greater poetry if the court of James had remained in Edinburgh and he had written his poetry in Scots. But I write here of the history of Scottish poetry achieved, and that of Drummond is a notable achievement and not to be underestimated for reasons either of politics or literary theory.

The Union of the Crowns, like Flodden, has been seen as the day a blind came down on the Scots tradition in poetry, but of course that tradition still continues to this day. It is true, however, that apart from Drummond the immediate post-Union Scottish poets did not achieve major work. I believe this to be as much a matter of chance as of cultural circumstances. Poetry can flourish under the most harsh of political circumstances as the poets of twentieth-century Russia have shown. Whilst not ignoring the undermining of the Scots tradition by the Union of the Crowns or the Reformation that introduced a Bible in English into Lowland Scotland, it is my belief that if there had been a poet of genius alive in the seventeenth century in Scotland he would have responded as only major poets can, by making poetry from what was available to him in these unpropitious times; minor poets succumb in such times, major poets survive.

It may be that it was being said at the end of the seventeenth century, as twentieth-century critics were to say of the late nineteenth-century period, that the Scottish tradition had all but been extinguished. If that was so, the nadir of one century was followed by another of renaissance. The major poets of the eighteenth century who wrote in Scots were Allan Ramsay, Robert Fergusson and Robert Burns. Ramsay's poetry is of major importance within the confines of the Scots tradition; in a European context it is of little significance. That said, Allan Ramsay is one of the giants of the history of Scottish poetry; he changed the face of Scottish culture and led Scottish poetry towards the new heights that are to be seen in the work of Robert Burns. In saying that I do not diminish the poetry of Robert Fergusson who wrote during the period between Ramsay and Burns. His work is of major importance within the Scots tradition and his early death is one of the tragedies of Scottish literature. But when we turn to the poetry of Robert Burns we enter, as with Henryson in the fifteenth century, a poetry of a quite different order of achievement. It is the work of a mind that found its full expression only in poetry. His social position and the cultural attitudes of polite Scottish society in eighteenth-century Scotland forced the poet into attitudes that were not helpful to his writing; the cultural drive of his time was towards an acceptance of English as the language for polite society and for serious poetry. The eyes of cultivated Scotsmen were on London, although, paradoxically, whilst rejecting many of the old Scottish ways, including the Scots language, they were also proud to be Scots. Mostly this cultural paradox was destructive to creative work, but a genius such as Burns, who was firmly rooted in his native Scottish culture, was able to absorb English influences without being dominated by them. In this century many critics have regretted these English influences on his poetry and especially his use of Augustan English alongside his native Scots. I would suggest that this absorption of English forms, as with James I or Gavin Douglas, enabled Burns to achieve, in some of his greatest poems, a fusion of contrasting levels of language that is quite typical of the greatest poems of the Scots tradition. Again it is an extension of language that only a poet of the highest intelligence and sophistication could achieve.

The other major Lowland Scottish poet of the eighteenth century was James Thomson. He went to London and accepted his new role as an Englishman. He, like William Drummond, broke theoretical rules of the necessity for a poet to write in his mother tongue to achieve authentic utterance that unites emotion and intellect. I would suggest that the success which Thomson achieved lies in the fact that despite his rejection of the Scots language he remained well-rooted in the tradition of the poets who did write in that language. His uniqueness in the English tradition lies in his Scottishness and especially so in the earliest version of his 'Winter' from *The Seasons*.

If we turn to the third language of eighteenth-century Scotland – Gaelic – we find a poetry the equal of anything, Burns excepted, written in either Scots or English. The four major poets are Alexander MacDonald, Rob Donn, Duncan Ban Macintyre and William Ross. Perhaps for the first time in Scottish poetry we can see a Gaelic poetry that is of the same world – in poetic terms – as Lowland poetry. This is not to suggest that the Gaelic poets had rejected the traditions of the language in which they wrote. Indeed, the reverse is true; their poetry takes its strengths from that tradition. Alexander MacDonald was influenced by James Thomson in his nature poetry, but in these as in other perhaps greater poems he reveals a new flowering of a very old tradition. So also the nature poetry of Duncan Ban Macintyre is quite apart from anything in Scots or English. And the love poems of William Ross, whilst bearing comparison with those of Burns, are unique to Gaelic poetry. The world that Rob Donn reveals in his poems is of a social order quite apart from that of the Lowlands although revealing a unifying humanity.

The eighteenth century saw a flourishing of the Lowland ballad tradition as well as of the folk song tradition in general. This interest in collecting and printing material of the folk tradition was to become more pronounced in the nineteenth century and has continued into the twentieth.

The nineteenth century has been seen as the nadir of Scottish poetry, the main creative literary drive being revealed in the novel. Sir Walter Scott is, of course, a giant in European literature and he restored the idea of Scotland to a European readership. The Enlightenment can be said to have given Scotland an intellectual influence equal to that of any other nation – and these writers mostly lived in Scotland. In the nineteenth century Scotland turned towards provincialism and those who would escape it went to London. Had they stayed in Scotland, of course, there might have been no provincialism.

Sir Walter Scott's poetry was in its day as widely read as his novels were later to be, but is little read now. His great contemporary, Byron, remains of major importance with his Scottish roots to be seen in the dramatic extremes of his work. The most important poet living in Scotland at that time was James Hogg whose poetry is being increasingly recognised today as of major importance, in the same way that his novel *The Private Memoirs and Confessions of a Justified Sinner* is also seen as a unique and important work. By the end of the century the poets were following the example of Carlyle and going to London. They wrote in English and fully accepted the idea that their work belonged to English poetry. The important London Scots were James Thomson ('B.V.') and John Davidson. The Scots-writing poets were without exception utterly provincial – of the kailyard – and of low ambition, knowing nothing of the major Scots poets apart from their idol, Robert Burns.

By the end of the nineteenth century, the Scottish tradition in poetry seemed to have come to an end but, as in previous times, it was a low before a high. In the 1920s a poet emerged who was recognised as being of major importance. I refer to Hugh MacDiarmid whose Scots poetry initiated what has been termed the Scottish Renaissance – a period of remarkable achievement by poets in all three languages of Scotland – Gaelic, Scots and English – and, as I indicated at the beginning of this Introduction, in varied mixtures of Scots and English. For the first time since the poetry of Robert Burns Scottish poetry had been returned to a worthy – and quite unprovincial – place amongst the poetry of Europe.

I have attempted here and in what follows to avoid exaggerated claims for the work that I introduce, but I would here suggest that the greatest achievement of the Scottish people is in their poetry.

SECTION I
Background Studies

A. DICTIONARIES

1 *The Illustrated Gaelic-English Dictionary*, compiled by Edward Dwelly. First published in parts 1901–11. Available now, Glasgow, Gairm Publications, latest reprint 1988.
Edward Dwelly is one of those heroes of what I can only describe as civilisation, who work fanatically to achieve their cultural ends. He hand-set the type for this massive work, and did so seated, unlike the professional compositors throughout typesetting history. He produced the parts of his dictionary single-handed not only with regard to the printing but in enlisting material from Gaelic speakers. I say single-handed but the exception to that was his wife. In a Preface to the second edition he wrote, 'I am also indebted to my wife for revising proofs, assisting in folding sheets, and preparing parts for post, as well as for advising many translations.'

2 *The New English-Gaelic Dictionary*, ed. Derick S. Thomson, Glasgow, Gairm Publications, 1981. Third impression 1990.

3 *The Concise Scots Dictionary*, editor-in-chief Mairi Robinson, Aberdeen, Aberdeen University Press, 1985. Paperback 1987.
There is an essay 'A History of Scots' by A. J. Aitken. This work may be concise but it is a most notable achievement, as well as a commercial success. See also no. 37. The concise dictionary is based on these major works of scholarship: *A Dictionary of the Older Scottish Tongue from the Twelfth Century to the end of the Seventeenth*, eds. William Craigie 1925–55, A.J. Aitken 1955–86 and James A.C. Stevenson 1973–85; continues (various editors)–*The Scottish National Dictionary [18th century to today]*, eds. William Grant 1929–46, David Murison 1946–76, completed in ten volumes, 1931–76.
The above three dictionaries, which are so varied in the means through which they were researched and published, are a vindication of the belief that languages and native cultures survive because they are at the root of individual lives within a varied national culture.

B. BIBLIOGRAPHIES

4 Duncan Glen, *A Bibliography of Scottish Poets from Stevenson to 1974*, Preston, Akros Publications, 1974.
5 Donald John Macleod, *Twentieth Century Publications in Scottish Gaelic*, Edinburgh, Scottish Academic Press, 1980.
6 W.R. Aitken, *Scottish Literature in English and Scots: A Guide to Information Sources*, Detroit, Gale Research Company, 1982.
7 Walter Scheps and J. Anna Looney, *Middle Scots Poets: A Reference Guide to James the First of Scotland, Robert Henryson, William Dunbar and Gavin Douglas*, Boston, Mass., G.K. Hall, 1986.

C. GENERAL HISTORIES OF SCOTLAND

8 *The Edinburgh History of Scotland*, 4 Volumes, Edinburgh, Oliver & Boyd, 1965–75.
   (a) Archibald A.M. Duncan, *Scotland: The Making of the Kingdom*, 1975. Latest paperback edition, Edinburgh, Mercat Press, 1989.
   (b) Ranald Nicholson, *Scotland: The Later Middle Ages*, 1965. Latest paperback edition, Edinburgh, Mercat Press, 1989.
   (c) Gordon Donaldson, *Scotland: James V to James VII*, 1965. Latest paperback edition, Edinburgh, Mercat Press, 1987.
   (d) William Ferguson, *Scotland: 1689 to the Present*, 1968. Latest paperback edition, Edinburgh, Mercat Press, 1987.
9 Rosalind Mitchison, *A History of Scotland*, London, Methuen, 1970. Second edition 1982. Paperback.

D. SOCIAL HISTORIES OF SCOTLAND

10 T.C. Smout, *A History of the Scottish People 1560–1830*, London, Collins, 1969. Fontana Paperback edition, 1972, many reprints, latest 1987.
11 T.C. Smout, *A Century of the Scottish People 1830-1950*, London, Collins, 1986. Fontana Press Paperback edition, 1987, and reprinted 1988.
12 Rosalind Mitchison, *Life in Scotland*, London, Batsford, 1978.

E. GENERAL BACKGROUND STUDIES

13 David Craig, *Scottish Literature and the Scottish People, 1680-1830*, London, Chatto & Windus, 1961.

14 George Elder Davie, *The Democratic Intellect: Scotland and her Universities in the Nineteenth Century*, Edinburgh, Edinburgh University Press, 1961. Paperback edition, 1981.
The classic and essential account of the generalist tradition of Scottish university education.

15 A.M. Kinghorn, *The Chorus of History: Literary-historical Relations in Renaissance Britain*, London, Blandford Press, 1971.

16 David Daiches, *Literature and Gentility in Scotland*, Edinburgh, Edinburgh University Press, 1982. The Alexander Lectures at the University of Toronto, 1980.

17 *A Companion to Scottish Culture*, ed. David Daiches, London, Edward Arnold, 1981.

18 John MacQueen, *Progress and Poetry, Volume I, The Enlightenment and Scottish Literature*, Edinburgh, Scottish Academic Press, 1982.

19 *The Companion to Gaelic Scotland*, ed. Derick S. Thomson, Oxford, Blackwell, 1983. Paperback edition 1987.
A pioneering book that has opened up a modern view of Gaelic culture and life to a wide audience.

20 Trevor Royle, *The Macmillan Companion to Scottish Literature*, London, Macmillan, 1983. Paperback edition 1984.
An alphabetical listing that covers a wide range of authors and subjects most accurately and with an open-minded approach to all aspects of Scottish literature.

21 George Elder Davie, *The Crisis of the Democratic Intellect: The Problem of Generalism and Specialisation in Twentieth-Century Scotland*, Edinburgh, Polygon, 1986.

22 Kenneth Simpson, *The Protean Scot: The Crisis of Identity in Eighteenth Century Scottish Literature*, Aberdeen, Aberdeen University Press, 1988.

F. HISTORIES OF SCOTTISH LITERATURE

23 J.H. Millar, *A Literary History of Scotland*, London, T. Fisher Unwin, 1903.
Amazingly it has not been quite superseded in its general statements, although of course the details and attitudes are not of our century, nor of the new world that is Scottish literary studies after a century of 'renaissance' of cultural identity in all aspects of Scottish life.

24 Sydney Goodsir Smith, *A Short Introduction to Scottish Literature*, Edinburgh, Serif Books, 1951.
A brief work by a poet involved in the battle for a modern Scottish

Literary Renaissance. It can still stimulate, not least in the bibliography.

25 Maurice Lindsay, *History of Scottish Literature*, London, Robert Hale, 1977.
A one-man history full of good insights.

26 Roderick Watson, *The Literature of Scotland*, London, Macmillan, 1984. Macmillan History of Literature.

27 *The History of Scottish Literature*, general editor Cairns Craig.

(a) *The History of Scottish Literature, Volume I, Origins to 1660 (Mediaeval and Renaissance)*, ed. R.D.S. Jack, Aberdeen, Aberdeen University Press, 1988. Paperback edition 1989.
Essays on poetry and on language are:
   (i)   Alex Agutter, 'Middle Scots as a Literary Language'.
   (ii)   M.P. McDiarmid, 'The Metrical Chronicles and Non-alliterative Romances'.
   (iii) Felicity Riddy, 'The Alliterative Revival'.
   (iv)   John MacQueen, 'Poetry - James I to Henryson'.
   (v)   Priscilla Bawcutt, 'William Dunbar and Gavin Douglas'.
   (vi)   Alasdair A. MacDonald, 'Religious Poetry in Middle Scots'.
   (vii) Gregory Kratzmann, 'Sixteenth-Century Secular Poetry'.
   (viii) R.D.S. Jack, 'Poetry Under King James VI'.
   (ix)   Michael Spiller, 'Poetry after the Union 1603–1660'.
   (x)   James Macqueen, 'Scottish Latin Poetry'.
   (xi)   W. Gillies, 'Gaelic: The Classical Tradition'.
   (xii) Hamish Henderson, 'The Ballad and Popular Tradition to 1660'.

(b) *The History of Scottish Literature, Volume II, 1660–1800.* ed. Andrew Hook, Aberdeen, Aberdeen University Press, 1987. Paperback edition 1989
Essays on poetry and song are:
   (i)   Alexander M. Kinghorn and Alexander Law, 'Allan Ramsay and Literary Life in the First Half of the Eighteenth Century'.
   (ii)   Mary Jane Scott, 'James Thomson and the Anglo-Scots'.
   (iii) Thomas Crawford, 'Lowland Song and Popular Tradition in the Eighteenth Century'.
   (iv)   F.W. Freeman, 'Robert Fergusson: Pastoral and Politics at Mid Century'.
   (v)   Derick S. Thomson, 'Gaelic Poetry in the Eighteenth Century'.
   (vi)   Carol McGuirk, 'Scottish Hero, Scottish Victim: Myths of Robert Burns'.

(c) *The History of Scottish Literature, Volume III, Nineteenth Century,* ed. Douglas Gifford, Aberdeen, Aberdeen University Press, 1989. Paperback edition 1989.

Essays on poetry are:

(i) Edwin Morgan, 'Scottish Poetry in the Nineteenth Century'.

(ii) John MacInnes, 'Gaelic Poetry in the Nineteenth Century'.

(d) *The History of Scottish Literature, Volume IV, Twentieth Century,* ed. Cairns Craig, Aberdeen, Aberdeen University Press, 1987. Paperback edition 1989.

Essays on poetry and song are:

(i) Colin Milton, 'Modern Poetry in Scots Before MacDiarmid'.

(ii) Ian A. Olson, 'Scottish Traditional Song and the Greig-Duncan Collection: Last Leaves or Last Rites?'.

(iii) Catherine Kerrigan, 'MacDiarmid's Early Poetry'.

(iv) Ritchie Robertson, 'Edwin Muir'.

(v) Terence McCaughey, 'Somhairle MacGill-Eain'.

(vi) Tom Hubbard, 'Reintegrated Scots: The Post- MacDiarmid Makars'.

(vii) Ronald I.M. Black, 'Thunder, Renaissance and Flowers: Gaelic Poetry in the Twentieth Century'.

(viii) Alan Riach, 'The Later MacDiarmid'.

(ix) Joy Hendry, 'Twentieth-century Women's Writing: The Nest of Singing Birds'.

(x) Roderick Watson, 'Internationalising Scottish Poetry'.

(xi) Barry Wood, 'Scots, Poets and the City'.

These four volumes are of major importance. Poetry dominates the first volume and is of major importance in Volume II but the paucity of poetry of major standing is revealed in Volume III although I believe that a discussion of this in background essays could have given this volume a better balance. Volume IV is the most 'journalistic' and lacks truly considered analysis in several of the essays, but it has the admirable quality of being without a doctrinaire viewpoint, which is surely proper for what must be a biased 'history' of what is still a living, political and creatively complex literature in three languages, with many variations within these languages not only of vocabulary but also of forms that demand a variety of responses. So, as Cairns Craig, editor not only of the fourth volume but general editor of all four volumes, says, it is to be hoped 'that the next year's creativity and the next decade's criticism will not only add to the creative wealth of the century's achievement in Scotland, but challenge and extend the perceptions which we have gathered here.'

G. LANGUAGES OF SCOTLAND

28 *Lowland Scots*, ed. A.J. Aitken, Edinburgh, Association for Scottish Literary Studies, 1973. Occasional Paper no.2.

29 David Murison, *The Guid Scots Tongue*, Edinburgh, William Blackwood, 1977.

30 *Languages of Scotland*, eds. A.J. Aitken and Tom McArthur, Edinburgh, Chambers, 1979. The Association for Scottish Literary Studies. Occasional Paper no.4.
Part 3 of this excellent book is 'The Study of Scotland's Languages'. It comprises, 'Papers on the current study of and investigations into Gaelic, Scots and Scottish standard English' by Donald MacAulay and A.J. Aitken. I draw particular attention to them for the extensive bibliographies appended.

31 *Scotland and the Lowland Tongue*, ed. J. Derrick McClure, Aberdeen, Aberdeen University Press, 1983.

32 Derick S. Thomson, *Why Gaelic Matters*, Edinburgh and Inverness, The Saltire Society and An Comunn Gaidhealach, 1984.

33 Charles W.J. Withers, *Gaelic in Scotland 1698–1981: The Geographical History of a Language*, Edinburgh, John Donald Publishers, 1984.

34 Billy Kay, *Scots: The Mither Tongue*, Edinburgh, Mainstream Publishing, 1986. Paperback edition, London, Grafton Books, 1988.

35 J. Derrick McClure, *Why Scots Matters*, Edinburgh, The Saltire Society and Scots Language Society, 1988.

36 *Gaelic and Scotland – Alba agus a' Ghàidhlig*, ed. William Gillies, Edinburgh, Edinburgh University Press, 1989.
A collection of essays covering literature and history as well as the status of Gaelic in Scotland today.

37 *The Scots Thesaurus*, eds. Iseabail Macleod with Pauline Cairns, Caroline Macafee and Ruth Martin, Aberdeen, Aberdeen University Press, 1990.
A work of major importance. It is an analysis of almost the entire content of Lowland Scots as published in no. 3 above and gives a unique insight into the life of Lowland Scotland from the late twelfth century to today.

H. GENERAL STUDIES OF SCOTTISH POETRY

38 *Scottish Poetry: a Critical Study*, ed. James Kinsley, London, Cassell,

1955.

Still the best one-volume introduction although, of course, out of date on many matters, and weak on Gaelic.

The essays are:

(i)   James Kinsley, 'The Mediaeval Makars'.

(ii)   Agnes Mure Mackenzie, 'The Renaissance Poets: (I) Scots and English'.

(iii)   James W.L. Adams, 'The Renaissance Poets: (II) Latin.

(iv)   Sir James Fergusson, 'The Ballads'.

(v)   A.M. Oliver, 'The Scottish Augustans'.

(vi)   David Daiches, 'Eighteenth-Century Vernacular Poetry'.

(vii)   Robert Dewar, 'Burns and the Burns Tradition'.

(viii) John W. Oliver, 'Scottish Poetry in the Earlier Nineteenth Century'.

(ix)   Douglas Young, 'Scottish Poetry in the Later Nineteenth Century'.

(x)   George Kitchin, 'The Modern Makars'.

There is also Douglas Young, 'A Note on Scottish Gaelic Poetry'.

39 Derick Thomson, *An Introduction to Gaelic Poetry*, London, Victor Gollancz, 1974. Paperback edition, Edinburgh, Edinburgh University Press, 1989.

This is the standard history of Gaelic poetry by a modern scholar; it is indispensable for today's reader.

40 *Bards and Makars, Scottish Language and Literature: Medieval and Renaissance*, eds. Adam J. Aitken, Matthew P. McDiarmid and Derick S. Thomson, Glasgow, University of Glasgow Press, 1977.

A most useful book with essays on a wide range of subjects including four essays on Robert Henryson, three on William Dunbar and one on three seventeenth-century Bardic Poets: Niall Mór, Cathal and Niall MacMhuirich. I refer to other essays later in this guide.

I. LITERARY CRITICISM AND THEORY

41 C.M. Grieve, *Contemporary Scottish Studies*, London, Leonard Parsons, 1926. Extended edition, Edinburgh, Scottish Educational Journal, 1976 which prints the correspondence these essays furiously aroused.

42 *Edinburgh Essays on Scots Literature*, Edinburgh, Oliver & Boyd, 1933.

43 Hugh MacDiarmid, *At the Sign of the Thistle: A Collection of Essays*, London, Stanley Nott, 1934.

44 Janet M. Smith, *The French Background of Middle Scots Literature*, Edinburgh, Oliver & Boyd, 1934.

45 Edwin Muir, *Scott and Scotland: The Predicament of the Scottish Writer*, London, Routledge, 1936. Reprinted, Edinburgh, Polygon, 1982, with an Introduction by Allan Massie.

46 John Speirs, *The Scots Literary Tradition: An Essay in Criticism*, London, Chatto & Windus, 1940; 2nd revised edition, London, Faber & Faber, 1962.

47 Kurt Wittig, *The Scottish Tradition in Literature*, Edinburgh, Oliver & Boyd, 1958. Reprinted Westport, Conn., Greenwood Press, 1972; reprinted Edinburgh, James Thin, Mercat Press, 1978.

48 Hugh MacDiarmid, *The Uncanny Scot*. ed. Kenneth Buthlay, London, MacGibbon & Kee, 1968.

49 Hugh MacDiarmid, *Selected Essays*, ed. Duncan Glen, London, Cape, 1969; Berkeley, California, University of California Press, 1970.

50 Duncan Glen, *The Individual and the Twentieth-Century Scottish Literary Tradition*, Preston, Akros Publications, 1971.

51 R.D.S. Jack, *The Italian Influence on Scottish Literature*, Edinburgh, Edinburgh University Press, 1972.

52 Edwin Morgan, *Essays*, Cheadle, Carcanet New Press, 1974. Five of the essays are reprinted in 62 below.

53 Edwin Muir, *Uncollected Scottish Criticism*. ed. Andrew Noble, London and Totowa, N.J., Vision and Barnes & Noble, 1982.

54 *Literature of the North*, eds. David Hewitt and Michael Spiller, Aberdeen, Aberdeen University Press, 1983.

55 Hugh MacDiarmid, *The Thistle Rises: An Anthology of Poetry and Prose*, ed. Alan Bold, London, Hamish Hamilton, 1984.

56 Somhairle Mac Gill-eain, *Ris a' Bhruthaich: Criticism and Prose Writings*, ed. William Gillies, Stornoway, Acair, 1985.

57 R.D.S. Jack, *Scottish Literature's Debt to Italy*, Edinburgh, Italian Institute and Edinburgh University Press, 1986.

58 Iain Crichton Smith, *Towards the Human: Selected Essays*, Edinburgh, Macdonald, 1986.

59 Edwin Muir, *Selected Prose*, ed. George Mackay Brown, London, John Murray, 1987.

60 Edwin Muir, *The Truth of Imagination: Some Uncollected Reviews and Essays*, ed. P.H. Butter, Aberdeen, Aberdeen University Press, 1988.

61 Robin Fulton, *The Way Words are Taken: Selected Essays*, Edinburgh, Macdonald, 1989.

62 Edwin Morgan, *Crossing the Border: Essays on Scottish Literature*, Manchester, Carcanet, 1990.

SECTION II
Anthologies and Magazines

A. ANTHOLOGIES

GENERAL

63 Moray McLaren, *The Wisdom of the Scots: a Choice and a Comment*, London, Michael Joseph, 1961.

This book has as much prose as poetry, but it is the first anthology of Scottish writing that I would put into the hands of someone coming new to Scottish culture; it excludes Gaelic work but McLaren is aware of Gaelic influences. Within the aims of this anthology the poetry selected is first-rate and Moray McLaren's urbane yet knowledgeable comments are very useful; in support he had the scholarly help of R.L. Lorimer.

GENERAL POETRY

64 *Leabhar na Féinne: Heroic Gaelic Ballads Collected in Scotland Chiefly from 1512 to 1871*, ed. J.F. Campbell, Shannon, Irish University Press, 1972. Photolithographic facsimile of the first edition, 1872. With a new Introduction by Derick S. Thomson.

65 *Bàrdachd Ghàidhlig: Gaelic Poetry 1550–1900*, ed. William J. Watson, Inverness, An Comunn Gaidhealach, 1976. Reprint of the third edition of 1959. First published in 1918.

66 *The Oxford Book of Scottish Verse*. eds. John MacQueen and Tom Scott, Oxford, Clarendon Press, 1966. Later editions with corrections 1975 and 1981. Paperback edition, with corrections, 1989.

Still the best anthology over the whole Lowland history, but it needs updating for the twentieth-century poets and there is no Gaelic which would, I hope, not happen today where the generalised term 'Scottish' is used.

67 *The Penguin Book of Scottish Verse*, ed. Tom Scott, Harmondsworth, Penguin, 1970. Reprinted several times.

Particularly useful for the Introduction by Tom Scott.

9

68 *Scottish Satirical Verse: an Anthology*, ed. Edwin Morgan, Manchester, Carcanet New Press, 1980.
    Covers the period from the earliest anonymous verse to Tom Leonard, born in 1944. No Gaelic verse.

FOURTEENTH TO SEVENTEENTH CENTURIES

69 *Bàrdachd Albannach o Leabhar Deadhan Lios-Mòir. Scottish Verse from the Book of the Dean of Lismore*, ed. William J. Watson, Edinburgh, Scottish Academic Press for the Scottish Gaelic Texts Society, 1978.
    Reprint of the first edition of 1937 which was Volume I of the Society's publications. Gaelic and English parallel text.

70 *Heroic Poetry from the Book of the Dean of Lismore*, ed. Neil Ross, Edinburgh, Oliver & Boyd for the Scottish Gaelic Texts Society, 1939. Gaelic and English parallel text.

71 *Late Medieval Scots Poetry. A Selection from the Makars and their Heirs down to 1610*, ed. Tom Scott, London, Heinemann, 1967.
    Interesting for the Introduction with its emphasis on the European links of the Scottish poets.

72 *Ballattis of Luve*, ed. John MacQueen, Edinburgh, Edinburgh University Press, 1970.
    An anthology of the Scottish courtly love lyric 1400–1570. The title is from a section of the Bannatyne Manuscript which is the early source of so many Scots poems. Professor MacQueen has given us not only a superb text but a decent printing of it with regard to line breaks and indentions. It is very well designed and printed and is an excellent source for the love poems of Alexander Scott, the auld makar.

73 *The Middle Scots Poets*, ed. A.M. Kinghorn, London, Edward Arnold, 1970.
    This selection is particularly good for the Henryson poems.

74 *A Choice of Scottish Verse 1470–1570*, eds. John and Winifred MacQueen, London, Faber & Faber, 1972.

75 *A Choice of Scottish Verse 1560–1660*, ed. R.D.S. Jack, London, Hodder & Stoughton, 1978. Also available in paperback.
    A first-rate anthology for this somewhat neglected period.

76 *The Poetry of the Stewart Court*, eds. Joan Hughes and W.S. Ramson, Canberra, Australian National University Press, 1982.
    The fullest modern anthology of poems from the Bannatyne Manuscript with excellent representation for Robert Henryson, William Dunbar, Alexander Scott and with three Gavin Douglas Prologues. The spelling of Scots is very faithful to older usages. The analysis of the design or editorial plan of the Manuscript is indispensable.

77 *Longer Scottish Poems, Volume I 1375–1650*, eds. Priscilla Bawcutt and Felicity Riddy, Edinburgh, Scottish Academic Press, 1987. Also paperback edition.
   A superb anthology not only for enjoyable reading but as a contribution to textual scholarship. The bibliographies are very useful for critical books and essays as well as for the editions of the poets' works. Poets whose work is included in this anthology but who are unlisted in this guide are Sir Gilbert Haye (f.1450–60) and the anonymous author of *The Taill of Rauf Coilyear*. A new edition of Haye's *The Buik of King Alexander the Conqueror* is ed. John Cartwright, 3 Volumes, Edinburgh, Scottish Text Society, 1986–. *The Taill of Rauf Coilyear* is in *Scottish Alliterative Poems*, ed. F.J. Amours, 2 Volumes, Edinburgh, Blackwood for the Scottish Text Society, 1892–7; a new Scottish Text Society edition edited by Elizabeth Walsh is forthcoming; for a facsimile of the only known copy as printed by Robert Lekpreuik at St Andrews in 1572 see Edinburgh, National Library of Scotland, 1966 with a Bibliographical Note by William Beattie.
78 *Cassette*
   Ten Medieval Makars, Glasgow, Scotsoun, SSC 021.
   A selection from the poetry of Barbour, James I, Hary, Douglas, Lyndsay, Maitland, Scott, Montgomerie, Hume and Boyd.

SEVENTEENTH TO NINETEENTH CENTURIES
79 *Sàr Orain. Three Gaelic Poems*, ed. A. Macleod, Glasgow, An Comunn Gaidhealach, 1933.
   Prints poems by Mary MacLeod, Alexander MacDonald and Duncan Ban Macintyre.
80 *Love, Labour and Liberty: The Eighteenth-century Scottish Lyric*, ed. Thomas Crawford, Cheadle, Carcanet, 1976.
   This, of course, includes many songs by Robert Burns, and there are twelve poems by Allan Ramsay and three by Robert Fergusson, but there are also many fine anonymous songs.
   The companion to this anthology is Thomas Crawford's *Society and the Lyric: a Study of the Song Culture of Eighteenth-Century Scotland*, Edinburgh, Scottish Academic Press, 1979.
81 *Longer Scottish Poems, Volume II 1650–1830*, eds. Thomas Crawford, David Hewitt and Alexander Law, Edinburgh, Scottish Academic Press, 1987. Also paperback edition.
   As with Volume I, 77 above, this is a superb book that is a scholarly yet very readable collection of poems with excellent introductions to the poets' works and, as with Volume I, very useful bibliographies.

Poets included in this anthology to whom I do not give a separate
listing in this guide are: William Cleland (?1661–1689); Lady
[Elizabeth] Wardlaw (1677–1727) represented by her famous fake
heroic ballad 'Hardyknute'; David Mallet (?1702–1765); William
Hamilton of Bangour (1704–1754); Adam Skirving (1719–1803)
represented by 'Tranent Muir' (his famous song 'Johnnie Cope' is in
the Tom Scott Penguin anthology); John Skinner (1721–1807) with
an imitation of 'Chrystis Kirk on the Grene' – he is better known for
his song 'Tullochgorum'; James Beattie (1735–1803); John Mayne
(1795–1836); and Charles Keith (died 1807).

NINETEENTH AND TWENTIETH CENTURIES

82 *Modern Scottish Poetry. An Anthology of the Scottish Renaissance
    1920–1945*, ed. Maurice Lindsay, London, Faber & Faber, 1946. The
    latest revised edition is, London, Robert Hale, 1986 and covers the
    period 1925–85.
    The first edition is a classic. The latest edition, although the
    anthology I would recommend as an introduction to twentieth-
    century Scottish poetry in Gaelic, Scots and English, is weak on
    many recent developments, particularly free forms of poetry in
    English and all forms in Scots since the sixties. Indeed, even earlier
    writers in Scots such as Robert Garioch and Tom Scott are
    under-represented; but so also, I believe, is William Montgomerie.
    We await a Lindsay of the nineties.

83 *Scottish Verse 1851–1951*, ed. Douglas Young, London, Nelson,
    1952.
    The only modern anthology to cover at all adequately the period
    from 1851 to the appearance of Hugh MacDiarmid in the twenties.
    Most of the poetry of the second half of the last century is poor but
    see 91 below.

84 *Twelve Modern Scottish Poets*, ed. Charles King, London, University
    of London Press, 1971. There are later editions of this very
    successful anthology but it has not been updated, although still a
    book of very good poetry.
    The poets represented are: Edwin Muir, Hugh MacDiarmid, William
    Soutar, George Bruce, Robert Garioch, Norman MacCaig, Sydney
    Goodsir Smith, Tom Scott, Edwin Morgan, Alexander Scott, George
    Mackay Brown and Iain Crichton Smith. The decision to omit poetry
    in Gaelic was a mistake which led to the exclusion of Sorley
    MacLean's poetry.

85 *Nua-bhàrdachd Ghàidhlig. Modern Scottish Gaelic Poems. A bilingual
    anthology*, ed. Donald MacAulay, Edinburgh, Southside, 1976. Latest
    paperback edition, Canongate, 1987.

This anthology of poetry of a remarkably high standard prints poems by Sorley MacLean, George Campbell Hay, Derick Thomson, Iain Crichton Smith and Donald MacAulay.

86   *Modern Scots Verse 1922–1977*, ed. Alexander Scott, Preston, Akros Publications, 1978.
This anthology reveals the high achievements of writers in Scots from MacDiarmid until 1977.

87   *Twelve More Modern Scottish Poets*, eds. Charles King and Iain Crichton Smith, London, Hodder & Stoughton, 1986.
The poets represented are: G.S. Fraser, George Campbell Hay, Maurice Lindsay, W.S. Graham, Derick Thomson, Alastair Mackie, Burns Singer, Stewart Conn, Douglas Dunn, Tom Leonard, Liz Lochhead and Valerie Gillies. This time, in contrast to 84 above, Gaelic poetry has been included.

88   *European Poetry in Scotland. An Anthology of Translations*, eds. Peter France and Duncan Glen, Edinburgh, Edinburgh University Press, 1989.
An anthology of twentieth-century translations with an extract from Gavin Douglas's translation of Virgil's *The Aeneid* as a Prologue to the modern work which begins with Sir Alexander Gray (born 1882) and ends with W.N. Herbert (born 1961).
See also the cassettes *Virgil, Dante, et al, Scots-Italian/Italiano-Scozzese*, Glasgow, Scotsoun, 1990, 2 tapes SSC 087, SSC 088. Scotsoun Euro-Makars series. Bilingual readings; many of the modern translations into Italian are taken from *La Nuova Poesie Scozzese*, eds. Duncan Glen and Nat Scammacca, Palermo, Celebes Editore, 1976.

89   *The Best of Scottish Poetry. An Anthology of Contemporary Scottish Verse*, ed. Robin Bell, Edinburgh, Chambers, 1989.
An anthology of poetry by living poets chosen by themselves and with an introduction by each poet to his or her work. Almost uniquely for a 'high art' anthologist, Robin Bell includes songs by Hamish Henderson, Ewan MacColl, Adam MacNaughtan and Midge Ure.

90   *Twenty of the Best. And Another for Good Measure. A Galliard Anthology of Contemporary Scottish Poetry*, ed. Duncan Glen, Edinburgh, Galliard, 1990. An anthology that focuses on younger poets writing in Gaelic, Scots and English who are not printed in 89 above but amongst the twenty-one poets are also older ones omitted from Robin Bell's anthology.

91   *Radical Renfrew. Poetry from the French Revolution to the First World War by poets born or sometimes resident in the County of Renfrewshire*, ed. Tom Leonard, Edinburgh, Polygon, 1990.

A pioneering work that reveals a new aspect of Scottish poetry in the nineteenth-century as William Donaldson's researches have done for prose-writing in the popular press; see Donaldson's essay in 27(c) above and his *Popular Literature in Victorian Scotland*, Aberdeen, Aberdeen University Press, 1986. Amongst the poets given a new recognition by Tom Leonard is the radical feminist Marion Bernstein (fl. 1876).

92 *Bàrdachd na Roinn-Eorpa an Gaidhlig. European Poetry in Gaelic*, ed. Ruaraidh MacThòmais, Glasgow, Gairm Publications, 1990.
An anthology of translations into Gaelic made over the last forty years, some two-thirds or so of them having first appeared in the magazine *Gairm*, see 96 below.

93 *An Aghaidh na Sìorraidheachd: Ochdnar Bhàrd Gàidhlig. In the Face of Eternity. Eight Gaelic Poets*, ed. Christopher Whyte, Edinburgh, Polygon, 1991.
A bilingual anthology of poetry by younger poets. The poets are Meg Bateman, Maoilios M. Caimbeul, Anne Frater, Fearghas MacFhionnlaigh, Aonghas MacNeacail, Catrìona NicGumaraid, Màiri NicGumaraid and Christopher Whyte.

94 *The New Makars. The Mercat Anthology of Contemporary Poetry in Scots*, ed. Tom Hubbard, Edinburgh, James Thin, The Mercat Press, 1991.
Prints many poets who have become known since Alexander Scott's anthology of 1987, no. 86 above, and also more recent work by poets who are in Scott's book.

B. CURRENT ANNUAL ANTHOLOGY

95 *New Writing Scotland*, various editors, Aberdeen, Association for Scottish Literary Studies, 1983– continuing. Annually.

C. TWENTIETH-CENTURY MAGAZINES

The revival of Scottish literature in this twentieth century will always be associated with the name of Hugh MacDiarmid, or C.M. Grieve, and the first major platform for his ideas on a 'Scottish Renaissance' was his monthly magazine *The Scottish Chapbook*, ed. C.M. Grieve, Montrose, C.M. Grieve, 1922–23. MacDiarmid edited other magazines in the twenties and also *The Voice of Scotland* (1938–39, 1945–49 and 1955–58) but the *Chapbook* is the most important of his magazines. In the thirties the important quarterly for poetry was *The Modern Scot*, ed. J. H. Whyte, Dundee (later St Andrews), 1930–36.

The important poetry magazine of the forties was *Poetry Scotland*, ed. Maurice Lindsay, Glasgow, Maclellan, 1943–49, four issues being published. In 1954 the Saltire Society launched *Saltire Review*, quarterly 1954–61, and *New Saltire*, 1961–64, succeeded it. *Scottish International*, 1968–740 was influential but poetry was not its primary interest. *Scotia Reviev*, ed. David Morrison was nothing if not polemical. The first long-running twentieth-century magazines that have been important to Scottish poetry and still survive are *Gairm*, which is concerned with all aspects of Gaelic culture and has been of major importance, and *Lines Review* equally important and solely concerned with poetry. Since the emergence of the Scottish Arts Council in the sixties as a major financial supporter of Scottish literary publishing, other magazines have flourished. New magazines appear all the time often with regional interests or specific language interests. A current example is *Scrievins*, ed. committee, Markinch, Fife Writers Group, 1985 – continuing.

96 *Gairm*, ed. Ruaraidh MacThòmais, Glasgow, Gairm Publications, 1952 – continuing. Quarterly.

97 *Lines Review*, various editors, currently (1990) Tessa Ransford, Edinburgh (later Loanhead), M. Macdonald, 1952 – continuing. Quarterly.

98 *Akros*, ed. Duncan Glen, Glasgow (later Preston and later again Nottingham), Akros Publications, 1965–83. Three issues a year.

99 *(New) Edinburgh Review*, various editors, currently (1990) Murdo Macdonald, Edinburgh, Edinburgh Review, 1969 – continuing. Originally monthly, now quarterly.

100 *Chapman*, various editors, currently (1990) Joy Hendry, Hamilton (later Edinburgh), Chapman, 1970 – continuing. Three a year.

101 *Lallans*, various editors, currently (1990) David Purves, Dunfermline (later Aberdeen), The Lallans Society (later re-named The Scots Language Society), 1973 – continuing. Two a year.

102 *Cencrastus*, various editors, currently (1990) Raymond Ross, Edinburgh, 1979 – continuing. Quarterly.

103 *Verse*, eds. Robert Crawford, Henry Hart and David Kinloch, Oxford (later Glasgow and later again St Andrews), 1984 – continuing. Quarterly.

D. TWENTIETH-CENTURY SCHOLARLY JOURNALS

104 *Scottish Gaelic Studies*, various editors, Oxford, Oxford University Press (later Oxford, Blackwell, and currently Aberdeen, University of Aberdeen), 1926 – continuing. Occasionally.

105 *Scottish Studies*, various editors, Edinburgh, School of Scottish Studies, Edinburgh University, 1957 – continuing. Annually. Concerned with folk literature.

106 *Studies in Scottish Literature*, ed. G. Ross Roy, Lubbock, Texas, Department of English, Texas Technological College (later, Columbia, University of Columbia), 1963 – continuing. Originally quarterly, now annually.

107 *Scottish Literary Journal*, various editors, Aberdeen, Association for Scottish Literary Studies, 1974 – continuing. Two issues a year and *Supplements* and *Scottish Language: An Annual Review*, 1982 – continuing.

The *Supplements* often contain an annual survey 'The Year's Work in Scottish Literary and Linguistic Studies'. See also 'The Annual Bibliography of Scottish Literature' published as a supplement to *The Bibliotheck*.

The Association for Scottish Literary Studies aims to promote the study, teaching and publication of Scottish literature. An annual volume is published and conferences arranged, the papers read at them sometimes being published .

SECTION III
The Auld Bards and Makars

A. BRITISH PRE-HISTORY

ANEIRIN (Sixth Century)
108 *The Gododdin. The Oldest Scottish Poem,* ed. Kenneth Hurlstone
Jackson, Edinburgh, Edinburgh University Press, 1969. Paperback
edition, 1978.
A prose version.
This great heroic poem is in Brythonic speech which, to quote from
Matthew P. McDiarmid's essay in *Scotland and the Lowland Tongue,*
31 above, is 'now represented only by Welsh but once spoken in
both Highlands and Lowlands, and around Glasgow as late as the
twelfth century'. Mr McDiarmid also writes of this great poem in his
essay in 27(a) above, describing it as 'the earliest extant of Europe's
heroic poems in a vernacular tongue, and for sensibility the best.
Only in our times has it been brought into Scots consciousness. One
can still respond to the human voice in it.' To make a creative verse
version of this great poem is a challenge awaiting a modern poet.

B. EARLY SCOTS POETRY

THOMAS RIMOUR OF ERCELDOUNE (*c.*1225–*c.*1300)
109 *The Romance and Prophecies of Thomas of Erceldoune,* ed. James A.H.
Murray, London, N. Trubner & Co. for the Early English Text
Society, 1875.
This edition gives five texts of the 'True Thomas' poem from which
original forms of this work can be created.
The name I give above is found in the dark world that surrounds so
many old Scottish bards and makars. He is sometimes accredited
with authorship of *Sir Tristrem*. The editors of *The Oxford Book of
Scottish Verse,* 66 above, do so when they print an extract from it as
the first poem of their anthology. For a first poem in a version of

17

the Scots language, taking a hint from Moray McLaren, I recommend you to his anthology, *The Wisdom of the Scots*, 63 above, for an excellent version of what became the ballad 'True Thomas', accredited in this earlier form to Thomas of Erceldoune. This is a grand beginning to any literature.

This is a tale of a vision of beauty – a supernatural woman – and of the poet surrendering to her and so being rewarded with the power of imagination; and with the power to give form to his vision; and in his poetry able to express the truth that is in all authentic beauty and poetry. In his anthology Moray McLaren writes that the concept of surrendering oneself to the truth of beauty 'is one strong element in the wisdom of the Scot'. This may not be a concept of the Scot that is popularly accepted but it is a true one nevertheless. For a discussion of 'The Relationship between *Thomas the Rhymer* and Thomas of Erceldoune' see the essay of that title by Emily B. Lyle in *Leeds Studies in English*, n.s. 4, 1970.

JOHN BARBOUR (c.1320–95)

110 *Barbour's Bruce*, eds. Matthew P. McDiarmid and James A.C. Stevenson, 3 Volumes, Edinburgh, Scottish Text Society, 1980–5.
111 *The Bruce. A Selection*, ed. Alexander Kinghorn, Edinburgh, Oliver & Boyd for The Saltire Society, 1960. The Saltire Classics.
112 *Cassette*
Extracts from the Brus, selected by Matthew P. McDiarmid, Glasgow, Scotsoun, 1978, SSC 041.

An epic such as the *Bruce* cries out to be read in full. It is written with an assurance which, to follow James Kinsley in his essay in 38 above, suggests that Barbour was working not only in an established European tradition but also within a Scottish one, the poems of which, like so much other early Scottish poetry, have been lost. The most famous passage in Barbour's epic is that beginning 'Ah, fredome is a noble thing' and although this is but a moment in this long national epic it is one in which the poet does throw off a detached stance and writes from the heart. But although Barbour may lack the passion of Hary in his epic *Wallace*, and draw back from facing the horrors of total war, he does by building up details in noble language to reveal what it was like to be there in a way that still involves us at a human level as we read.

113 A.M. Kinghorn, 'Scottish Historiography in the Fourteenth Century: A New Introduction to Barbour's *Bruce*', *Studies in Scottish Literature*, vol. 6, no. 3, January 1969.
114 Lois A. Ebin, 'John Barbour's *Bruce*: Poetry, History and Propaganda', *Studies in Scottish Literature*, vol. 9, no. 4, April 1972.

JAMES STEWART, JAMES I OF SCOTLAND (1394–1437)

115 *The Kingis Quair*, ed. Matthew P. McDiarmid, London, Heinemann, 1973. This edition has an excellent Introduction and I recommend it for that reason, but there is an equally good text edited by John Norton-Smith, Oxford, Clarendon Press, 1971, revised 1981.
Earlier editions include: Walter W. Skeat's, Edinburgh, Scottish Text Society, 1884, 2nd revised edition 1911; and W. Mackay Mackenzie's, London, Faber & Faber, 1939.

This is a poem of wondrous complications with roots in *De Consolatione Philosophiae* of Boethius and concerned with the support and confidence to be received from a philosophy based on the wonder that is love. This is the philosophy of a love poetry that grows out of personal experience which included the poet's past, during which he suffered many years of imprisonment in England. Also, although this is a poem of the highly-literary courtly style, it is also a poem of courtship and a love that leads to marriage. The *Quair* has been seen by some critics, including C.S. Lewis in his *The Allegory of Love*, 1936, as the poem in which the poetry of marriage emerges from the poetry of adultery acceptable in *amour courtois*. For all the wonder of the dream-vision and the complexity of the art of this poem which matches the complexity of the world, whether medieval or modern, this is not only the narrative of the development of a mind in philosophical terms but also a poem of a real man and a real love and real life, or as Matthew P. McDiarmid says in his Introduction to 115 above, it is 'a spiritual autobiography'. An old tradition had indeed been made new; as poetry, *The Kingis Quair* is as fresh and alive today as when written in, say, 1435.

116 Andrew von Hendy, 'The Free Thrall: A Study of *The Kingis Quair*', *Studies in Scottish Literature*, vol. 2, no. 3, January 1965.

117 Ian Brown, 'The Mental Traveller – A Study of *The Kingis Quair*', *Studies in Scottish Literature*, vol. 5, no. 4, April 1968.

118 Tom Scott, 'The Long Poem: A Reading of *The Kingis Quair*', *Chapman*, no. 30, Summer 1981.

For a brief introduction to numerological features or 'felicities' in *The Kingis Quair* see John MacQueen's essay 'Poetry – James I to Henryson' in *The History of Scottish Literature, Volume II*, 27(a) above.

ANONYMOUS FIFTEENTH CENTURY

119 *Colkelbie Sow*
A whole anthology could be compiled under this heading, but I insert it to draw particular attention to 'Colkelbie Sow' (c.1470). There is an extract from it in the MacQueen/Scott anthology, 66

above, but the poem does demand to be read in full. It is printed in full in *The Poetry of The Stewart Court*, 76 above, and there is an equally good text, with a long introduction to the poem, in *'Colkelbie Sow' and 'The Talis of Fyve Bestes'*, ed. Gregory Kratzmann, New York and London, Garland Publishing, 1983. Garland Medieval Texts. For some readers it may be more convenient to refer to *The Bannatyne Manuscript*, ed. W. Tod Ritchie, Vol. IV, Edinburgh, Blackwood for the Scottish Text Society, 1930, pp. 279–96.

An old book, but a treasure-house of the anonymnous poems such as 'Colkelbie Sow', is David Laing's *Select Remains of the Ancient Popular and Romance Poetry of Scotland*, ed. J. Small, 1885; ed. W. Carew Hazlitt, 1895.

'Colkelbie Sow' is typical of the comic tradition to be seen throughout the history of Scottish poetry; a tradition of wild abandon quite at variance with the world's view of the cautious and dour Scot although, as the editors of *The Poetry of The Stewart Court*, 76 above, say of 'Colkelbie Sow', 'There is a profound seriousness underneath the foolery'.

It may be appropriate here to pay tribute to the many scholars who did pioneering work in the last century and early years of this century in editing the texts of our great poets, particularly Walter W. Skeat (Barbour and *The Kingis Quair*), G. Gregory Smith (Henryson), John Small (Dunbar and Gavin Douglas), W. Tod Ritchie (The Bannatyne Manuscript), William Craigie (Maitland Manuscript), James Cranstoun (Montgomerie) – and many others, not least David Laing whom I mention above. The Scottish Text Society has been of major importance in publishing many of these scholars' texts but the pioneering work of the publishing clubs should not be forgotten – the Bannatyne Club of which Sir Walter Scott was President and David Laing Secretary, the Maitland Club and the Hunterian Club.

RICHARD HOLLAND (c.1415–c.1482)

120 *The Buke of the Howlat*

For a modern text of Holland's poem see *Longer Scottish Poems, Volume I*, 77 above. It is also in *Scottish Alliterative Poems*, ed. F.J. Amours, 2 Volumes, Edinburgh, Blackwood for the Scottish Text Society, 1892–7.

A new Scottish Text Society edition is forthcoming.

The *Longer Scottish Poems* anthologists state that *The Buke of the Howlat* 'is the earliest substantial poem of the alliterative revival in Scotland' and in her essay in 27(a) above Felicity Riddy writes that the poem 'seems to contain the seeds of almost all the other alliterative poetry written in Scotland.' In his 'Introduction' to the Bannatyne Club edition of 1823 David Laing writes that the poem has been regarded 'without much injustice, as a prolix and very uncouth performance'. Until, say, the last twenty years the poem was seen as disjointed and incoherent but we see it differently today and indeed, to agree with an agreement, as the editors of *Longer Scottish Poems, Volume I* say, 'Recent criticism has emphasized the poem's coherence, and it seems sensible to agree with M.P. McDiarmid that it gives expression in a variety of ways to the themes of order and harmony, natural, social and political'. This is, of course, a very medieval poem but to modern readers, with the modernist movement in poetry behind us, we can perhaps accept the movement of that medieval poet's mind better than could some earlier 'modern' readers. I would not wish to claim too much for Holland's poem but the editors of *Longer Scottish Poems* perform a very valuable service by making what was not an easily available poem readily accessible, and so encouraging further recognition of its worth.

121 Matthew P. McDiarmid, 'Richard Holland's *The Buke of the Howlat*: an Interpretation', *Medium Aevum*, vol. 38, 1969.

122 Margaret A. Mackay, 'Structure and Style in Richard Holland's *The Buke of the Howlat*' in *Proceedings of the Third International Conference on Scottish Language and Literature (Medieval and Renaissance)*, eds. Roderick J. Lyall and Felicity Riddy, Glasgow, Department of Scottish Literature, University of Glasgow, 1981.

123 Flora Alexander, 'Richard Holland's *Buke of the Howlat*', in *Literature of the North*, eds. David Hewitt and Michael Spiller, Aberdeen, Aberdeen University Press, 1983.

ANONYMOUS

124 *Chrystis Kirk on the Grene*
This is one of the great popular Scottish poems which has been very influential on poets down the centuries. Although so popular it was, as many have said, obviously written by a very skilled poet and a cultured man, perhaps of high position, observing the ordinary people of Scotland with joy and pleasure, but without patronising them. I read it for its celebration of communal, popular conviviality, although I do not quite ignore the technical skill of the poet. It is my belief that it was written by James I, not James V, but no-one knows and truly it does not now matter, but if you are interested in academic argument for the case against its being by James I see Rev. Walter W. Skeat's Introduction to his Scottish Text Society edition of *The Kingis Quair*, 1911, and not least for his quotation from a

nineteenth-century critic: 'one can hardly suppose those critics serious, who attribute this song [Chrystis Kirk] to the moral and sententious James the First'. Whatever James may have been as a King, this is not the poet I know from reading *The Kingis Quair*.

'Chrystis Kirk' is printed in the MacQueen/Scott anthology, 66 above, and many other collections. Allan Ramsay's extended version, printed in *Longer Scottish Poems, Volume II*, 81 above, is interesting.

125 Allan H. MacLaine, 'The *Christis Kirk* Tradition: Its Evolution in Scots Poetry to Burns', in four parts, *Studies in Scottish Literature*, vol. 2, nos. 1–4, July 1964–April 1965.

126 *Peblis to the Play*
A poem often paired with 'Chrystis Kirk on the Grene'.

HARY (*c*.1440–92)

127 *Hary's 'Wallace'*, ed. Matthew P. McDiarmid, 2 Volumes, Edinburgh, Blackwood for the Scottish Text Society, 1968–9.
This is a very good edition and I recommend it for the long read that I believe a work such as this requires. It is a great patriotic work, of course, and a powerful influence on generations of Scots, even if only in stories told in the primary school. Too often critics have under-estimated Hary's skill as a poet and seen him as crude and unsubtle, but it is his direct realism that appeals to a modern reader. He does not romanticise war, knowing it to be bloody. In the Introduction to his edition of Hary above, Matthew P. McDiarmid writes, 'It is just this intensity of involvement in his uncomfortable and quite unknightly subject-matter that distinguishes him from, and makes him superior to, previous heroic poets.' And in his essay in 27(a) above, Mr McDiarmid writes of Hary's Wallace, 'So great a figure, so inwardly conceived, had not appeared in European literature. Not till the tragedies of Shakespeare would one personage so dominate the stage of imagination.'

C. THREE GREAT AULD MAKARS

ROBERT HENRYSON (*c*.1420–*c*.1490)

128 *The Poems of Robert Henryson*, ed. Denton Fox, Oxford, Clarendon Press, 1981. Oxford English Text series.
This is one of the finest fruits of the continuing modern interest in scholarly texts of Scottish poets. The massive Scottish Text Society edition edited by G. Gregory Smith, 3 Volumes 1906–14, printed varying texts from ten early sources. The 1981 edition by Professor

Fox gives us a superb critical text which is the end-product of intelligent scholarship of the highest order. The Introduction, over one hundred pages of captivating reading, is very much concerned with these textual matters and in some three hundred pages of Commentary the interest of even a non-specialist such as myself never flags as insight after insight is most stylishly made available to us, not only illuminating the poems but also the world and the literature that were part of Henryson's reality.

There is a revised and shortened paperback edition, 1987.

129 *Robert Henryson: The Poems and Fables,* ed. H. Harvey Wood, Edinburgh, Oliver & Boyd, 1933. Second revised edition 1958. Reprinted Edinburgh, James Thin, The Mercat Press, 1978.

Sections of the Introduction, inevitably, are now dated and the annotation in the Commentary is, again inevitably after the many advances in Scots scholarship in the last fifty years, inadequate by today's standards. But the text was a notable achievement in the early thirties by the young Harvey Wood who discovered the important Thomas Bassandyne print of 1571 and so his edition was the first to use that textual source.

130 *Poems,* ed. Charles Elliott, Oxford, Clarendon Press, 2nd edition, 1974. First published in 1963. Latest reprint 1987. Clarendon Medieval and Tudor series.

131 *Henryson,* selected by Hugh MacDiarmid, Harmondsworth, Penguin Books, 1973. Poet to Poet. Reprinted. Reveals MacDiarmid's interest in Henryson *and* Dunbar.

132 *Cassettes*

Poems of Robert Henryson, selected by Matthew P. McDiarmid, Glasgow, Scotsoun, 1975. SSC 018, 019. Two tapes.

With the poetry of Robert Henryson we enter a world of poetry that rises to heights of creativity and craftsmanship not previously discerned in the Scots tradition. With Henryson, as James Kinsley writes in his essay in 38 above, 'we enter a new world of poetry. Scottish poetry retained the muscular virtues of the earlier poets; but Henryson added new artistic qualities. He extended the bridgehead of cultivated style established by the author of *The Kingis Quair.*' At one time Henryson was described as one of the Scottish Chaucerians. This was, of course, an example of literary Imperialism imposed by the upholders of English literary tradition upon the Scots tradition, but we should not let nationalistic fervour mask us to the lessons that Henryson learned from the English master poet. Perhaps, apart from a movement between levels of language and tone, what the Scot learned most from Chaucer was, in an echo from Hugh MacDiarmid, 'Be yoursel!'. Or, as Professor Kinsley writes,

Henryson learned from Chaucer how to master 'the art of mirroring his own personality in his work'.

Henryson is a poet whose warm, kind and humorous personality comes across the divide of centuries through his great and varied poetry. In tone it has the range of a major poet and lacks nothing in rhetoric or grandiloquence when required, but for me his highest achievements are, paradoxically, attained in a lower key that is often colloquial. There, of course, I reveal a personal bias and don my prejudiced poet's hat. The greatness of 'The Testament of Cresseid' requires no substantiation by me but I believe that his *Fabillis* are perhaps a more unique achievement and equally great.

The supremely great quality of the *Fabillis* is their humour, allied to profound understanding of the humanity in man. It is a poetry that nevertheless does not undermine the essential animal qualities of the characters, whilst creating a tension between such qualities and those of humans. Alongside the homely language of, say, 'The Taill of the Uponlandis Mous and the Burges Mous' is revealed to us a major poet's high characterisation which is rich in homely yet sophisticated humour. In the terms of modern criticism this is a poem austere in its restraints in facing an imaginative reality but, of course, Henryson can write the conventionally ornate scene-setting of medieval poetry and is able to move from high rhetoric and learned statement to a more colloquial poetry as a means of sending up pomposity. This is the voice of a medieval Scot writing in a language which still exists. It has tones and attitudes that ring true to our twentieth-century Lowland Scottish ears; the ring of an authentic Scots that survives in a new form today in a Fife that has crossed many divides since the time of this great poet.

Each of us will have our favourites of these masterly fables. Without doubt one of the supreme achievements of Henryson is 'The Preiching of the Swallow'. It is a poem of great complexity; a poem of wisdom, as Moray McLaren reveals in his anthology, *The Wisdom of the Scots*, 63 above, as does John Burrow in his essay on this fable in *Essays in Criticism*, vol. 25, 1975, where he excellently indicates it as an 'ethical construction' of Prudentia and the Greek equivalent, 'Sophia', being both Divine Wisdom and the movement of the human mind which can achieve contact with the Divine Wisdom. Not for the first time I see in the medieval mind a reality that has become again important in this twentieth century, although of course all great poetry is concerned with ever-recurring truths and understandings. Not for nothing was Henryson's great successor in the Scots tradition, Hugh MacDiarmid, also concerned with the Divine Wisdom that is in the Greek Sophia and the Latin Prudence.

Other great fables by Henryson are 'The Taill of the Lyoun and the Mous' and 'The Taill of the Paddock and the Mous' which, with 'The Uponlandis Mous and the Burges Mous', reveal Henryson's unsurpassed use in major poetry of qualities that are in both mice and men whilst never ignoring that neither belongs in the same world. But it would be misleading to think that raising up a world of scampering mice suggests a quality of simplicity in these fables. All great poets reveal the ceremony of innocence, but they also reveal the movement of a wide and sophisticated intelligence, and by the unification of these seemingly opposing traits they create great poetry. In these fables there is no lack of range and if you wish both great humanitarian sensibilities and an awareness of the savagery that is in both man and animal, it can be seen here. I would suggest 'The Taill of the Wolf, the Fox and the Cadgear' as a good example.

The cutting edge of the humour underneath the powerful humanity of this great poetry should not be under-estimated. And in the swallow fable we have a description of Scottish landscape in winter that reveals another dimension to Henryson. As with many other poets, underneath the appreciation of pulsating life there is a rich response to the horror in both life and death. This is most famously to be seen in the great description of the leprosy that cursed Cresseid in Henryson's other masterpiece, 'The Testament of Cresseid'. This portrayal of horror is also to be seen in some of the fables and in the powerful images of the three skulls in 'The Thre Deid Pollis'. But in contrast we have the perfect light pastoral 'Robene and Makyne' with its varying moments of singing dialogue between lovers who although rustics speak to us in poetry of assured sophistication – and in a poetry uniquely Henrysonian in its tone and humanity.

'Robene and Makyne' is much anthologised, in, for example, 67, 71 and 73 above, the last, edited by Professor Kinghorn, being particularly good for poems by Henryson. I have referred to 'The Preiching of the Swallow' in McLaren, 63 above, and it is also in the MacQueen/Scott anthology, 66 above. In *Longer Scottish Poems, Volume I*, 77 above, the editors have included, with anglicised titles, 'The Two Mice', 'The Lion and the Mouse' and 'The Wolf, the Fox and the Cadger'. They also print 'The Testament of Cresseid', including 'The Complaint of Cresseid', as do 66, 67 and 73 above. One of the aims of G. Gregory Smith in editing Henryson for his edition at the beginning of this century was to make known a neglected poet. Now Robert Henryson's great poetry is recognised as one of the glories of Scotland.

133 Marshall W. Stearns, *Robert Henryson*, New York, Columbia
     University Press, 1949.
     Much research has followed but worth consulting.
134 John MacQueen, *Robert Henryson: A Study of the Major Narrative
     Poems*, Oxford, Clarendon Press, 1967.
135 John MacQueen, 'The Literature of Fifteenth-Century Scotland', in
     Scottish Society in the Fifteenth Century, ed. Jennifer M. Brown,
     London, Edward Arnold, 1977.
136 Douglas Gray, *Robert Henryson*, Leiden, E.J. Brill, 1979. Medieval and
     Renaissance Authors series.
137 Robert L. Kindrick, *Robert Henryson*, Boston, Twayne Publishers,
     1979. English Authors series.
138 Matthew P. McDiarmid, *Robert Henryson*, Edinburgh, Scottish
     Academic Press, 1981. Scottish Writers series.
139 Gregory Kratzmann, 'Henryson's *Fables*; 'the subtell dyte of poetry'',
     Studies in Scottish Literature, vol. 20, 1985.

WILLIAM DUNBAR (?1460–?1513)

140 *The Poems of William Dunbar*, ed. James Kinsley, Oxford, Clarendon
     Press, 1979. Oxford English Text series.
     A superb work of modern scholarship.
141 *The Poems of William Dunbar*, ed. W. Mackay Mackenzie, London,
     Faber & Faber, 1932, revised B. Dickins, 1960. Reprinted Edinburgh,
     James Thin, The Mercat Press, 1990.
     For long this was the standard edition of Dunbar's poetry for the
     modern reader. For textual scholarship and helpfulness to the reader
     through better glossary and notes it has been supplanted by the
     Kinsley edition listed above, but I suspect it will remain, for many
     of us, our favourite edition of William Dunbar.
142 *Selections from the Poems of William Dunbar*, ed. Hugh MacDiarmid,
     Oliver & Boyd for The Saltire Society, 1952. The Saltire Classics.
143 *Cassette*
     Poems of William Dunbar, selected by Edwin Morgan, Glasgow,
     Scotsoun, 1975, SSC 020.
     Dunbar is a poet who is diverse in his forms and the moods and
     responses that reflect these. He is a master of the short poem that
     is a virtuoso statement standing as a self-contained work of art. Each
     poem is superbly alive in its unique crafted singleness. So I believe
     that we need a wide-ranging selection of his poems. A favourite one
     day is replaced by another the next day or the next year. This is a
     poet of wide range. There is the satire of, for example, 'To the
     Merchantis of Edinburgh'; the descriptive 'Meditatioun in Wyntir';
     the many courtly poems such as 'The Thrissill and the Rois'

Goldyn Targe' with its superb opening description of a May morning which, in the words of the editor of *Longer Scottish Poems Volume I*, is 'a tour de force of jewelled imagery and 'aureate' language'. And if that is not enough there is 'The Tretis of the Twa Mariit Wemen and the Wedow' which for ever and a day should reveal that in Dunbar's time, as in ours, the Scot is not, sometimes, so puritanical as he is in caricature. Not alone in this but superbly so, Dunbar shows that the poets were Freudian in their perceptions before Freud, that destructive genius, created his powerful images. What Maurice Lindsay, in 25 above, excellently termed Dunbar's 'verbal fireworks' and 'erratic passion' make him for many the most exciting of all the Scottish poets.

144 J.W. Baxter, *William Dunbar: A Biographical Study*, Edinburgh, Oliver & Boyd, 1952.

145 Edwin Morgan, 'Dunbar and the Language of Poetry', *Essays in Criticism*, vol. 2, no. 2, April 1952. Reprinted in *Essays*, Cheadle, Carcanet Press, 1974 and *Crossing the Border*, Manchester, Carcanet, 1990.

146 Tom Scott, *Dunbar: A Critical Exposition of the Poems*, Edinburgh, Oliver & Boyd, 1966.

147 Priscilla Bawcutt, 'Aspects of Dunbar's Imagery' in *Chaucer and Middle English Studies*, ed. Beryl Rowland, London, Allen & Unwin, 1974.

148 Edmund Reiss, *William Dunbar*, Boston, Twayne Publishers, 1979.

149 Ian Simpson Ross, *William Dunbar*, Leiden, E.J. Brill, 1981. Medieval and Renaissance Authors series.

150 Pamela M. King, 'Dunbar's *The Golden Targe*: A Chaucerian Masque', *Studies in Scottish Literature*, vol. 19, 1984.

GAVIN DOUGLAS (c.1475–1522)

151 *Virgil's 'Aeneid' Translated into Scottish Verse by Gavin Douglas, Bishop of Dunkeld*, ed. David F.C. Coldwell, 4 Volumes, Edinburgh, Blackwood for the Scottish Text Society, 1957–64.

152 *Gavin Douglas: A Selection from his Poetry*, ed. Sydney Goodsir Smith, Edinburgh, Oliver & Boyd for The Saltire Society, 1959. The Saltire Classics.

153 *The Shorter Poems of Gavin Douglas*, ed. Priscilla J. Bawcutt, Edinburgh, Blackwood for the Scottish Text Society, 1967.
    Prints three poems, 'The Palice of Honour', 'Conscience' and 'King Hart'.

154 *Selections from Gavin Douglas*, ed. David F.C. Coldwell, Oxford, Clarendon Press, 1964.

155 *Cassette*

Extracts from Eneados and The Palice of Honour, selected by Matthew
P. McDiarmid, Scotsoun, 1978. SSC 042.
Like most 'modern' readers of Gavin Douglas I began with the
Prologues to his translation of Virgil's *Aeneid.* The most admired of
these are the so-called 'Nature Prologues' (VII, XII and XIII). It may,
indeed, be wise to begin with these. Since the eighteenth century
Douglas has been hailed in these Prologues as the first great
vernacular poet to be truly a masterly describer of the natural world
both panoramically and in close-up detail. Prologue VII on winter
has been particularly admired, perhaps *especially* so by Scots who
know the reality. But the long first day of summer of the twelfth
Prologue, 'hailsum May', is truly a luxuriant nature poem unlike the
more personal stance of the seventh Prologue, which Priscilla
Bawcutt has shrewdly suggested would be better titled 'Poet in a
wintry landscape' rather than 'Winter'; and Mrs Bawcutt sees
Prologue XIII, for all its beautiful description of a June night, as
'primarily a frame for the dreaming poet'. This is a useful response
to these poems in that it shows Douglas to be much more complex
as a poet in the Prologues than many critics have recognised. Of
course the same applies to James Thomson and, even more so, to
Robert Burns with regard to this question of the complexity of
seemingly straight description, or *real* reality, or anthology pieces
extracted because they are *really real* and *beautifully beautiful*
description. But none of this is to underestimate the beauty of the
descriptive sections of Douglas's great Nature Prologues nor their
remarkable range both metrically and in tone and subject.

The four-volume edition, three volumes of text, of Douglas's
Eneados may look an intimidating work, and critics are not difficult to
find who believe that interest in the classics is now declining. Of course,
with less importance attached to them in the schools and universities,
the position of Latin and Greek in our culture has altered, but interest in
the great literary works in Latin and Greek is on the upswing. And so
also their continuing importance is recognised as not an Imperial force
of Rome or of the English Empire but as a repository of fundamental
truths and beauty in great poetry. Ovid is now being read perhaps
more than ever before in this century for the good reason that he wrote
great poetry, and poetry that seems particularly relevant to us towards
the end of the twentieth century when our means of communication
give us a new metamorphosis. And so also are the great tales, such as
Virgil's *Aeneid,* important to us.

As always, I believe that a long poem demands to be read as a
single structured and unified creation — extracts give us another
work of art no matter how great they may be. The essence of the

work is destroyed by filleting it. Gavin Douglas's translation of Virgil may not be, as Ezra Pound proclaimed, greater than the original, but it is one of the greatest achievements of Scottish poetry – and one of the great translations of world literature. To read only the great and beautiful Prologues is to forfeit a great work of profound significance.

The essay by Priscilla Bawcutt 'William Dunbar and Gavin Douglas' in *The History of Scottish Literature Volume I*, 27(a) above, contains what I have quoted above by her.

156 Penelope Schott Starkey, 'Gavin Douglas's *Eneados*: Dilemmas in the Nature Prologues', *Studies in Scottish Literature*, vol. 11, nos. 1–2, July–October 1973.

157 Priscilla Bawcutt, *Gavin Douglas: A Critical Study*, Edinburgh, Edinburgh University Press, 1976.

The poetry and translations of Douglas are both intellectually and emotively a linguistic joy; in this book these qualities are not swamped despite the excellent scholarship.

D. ANONYMOUS POETRY IN GAELIC AND SCOTS

I insert this heading here largely to draw attention to the long anonymous years of Gaelic poetry. Most of it was communicated orally by the bards and James Macpherson's 'creations' made echoes of this poetry famous throughout Europe. But we want the genuine poetry. A useful beginning can be made with the large selection *Leabhar na Féinne*, 64 above, which takes us back a long way although not collected until the nineteenth century, and the language is not easy, even, I imagine, for those whose mother tongue is Gaelic. I also list two works which print poems from *The Book of the Dean of Lismore*, 69 and 70 above. These books give insight into the years when Gaelic was the language in which the imagination of what is now Scotland was enshrined. To truly come to terms with this Gaelic tradition, we have to think ourselves back creatively to the first millenium AD. This, of course, means that we have to appreciate the Gaelic influence on our culture many centuries before either Scots or English entered our historical consciousness. For most Lowland Scots that tradition is heard only in echoes and fragments, but for all Scots, even when the Lowlanders deny it, the Gaelic centuries are a deep and powerful cultural influence. For a study which is not uncritical of this influence as it is portrayed by today's Scots see *The Gaelic Vision in Scottish Culture* by Malcolm Chapman, London, Croom Helm, 1978. For a scholarly essay on the classical tradition of early Gaelic poetry, see William Gillies's in 27(a) above, and also the same author's essay, 'Courtly and Satiric Poems in the Book of the Dean of Lismore', *Scottish Studies*, vol. 21, 1977.

Another reason for inserting this heading here was to make reference to anonymous poems in Scots. This is a very small body of work compared with the Gaelic tradition, and compared with what must have been written in Scots but is now lost. Nevertheless the poems I refer to in the Scots tradition are one of the joys of this period. There is a heading 'Four May Poems' in the MacQueen/Scott anthology, 66 above. The bringing together of these four anonymous poems under this heading may be a minor piece of editing, but nevertheless a brilliant grouping. They belong to an old European tradition but are no worse for that. They transmit tremendous joy.

For these poems, as with so much anonymous early poetry in Scots, and also so many of the known makars, we are indebted to the Bannatyne Manuscript which is one of the earliest great Scottish anthologies. It was perhaps completed during the last three months of 1568 when plague in Edinburgh had forced the young George Bannatyne to move to his father's estate in Forfarshire. We must give praise beyond words to George Bannatyne, Edinburgh merchant, for his monumental anthology. Sir Walter Scott wrote, truly if not quite accurately, of the young Bannatyne's 'courageous energy to form and execute the plan of saving the literature of a whole nation'.

As with so much else, we have cause to be grateful to Allan Ramsay in the eighteenth century for being the first to print a large selection of poems from the Bannatyne Manuscript. He was loaned it in order to compile his collection of Scots verse, *The Ever Green*, 1724. I have referred, in 119 above, to the Scottish Text Society's 4-volume edition of the Manuscript, edited by W. Tod Ritchie, 1928–34, but some idea of the appearance of the manuscript can be gained from a facsimile edition superbly introduced by Denton Fox and William A. Ringler and published, London, Scolar Press with the National Library of Scotland, 1980. For other aspects of the design, or editing, of the Manuscript by Bannatyne see Joan Hughes and W.S. Ramson in their anthology, *The Poetry of the Stewart Court*, 76 above. Ramson writes 'On Bannatyne's Editing' in *Bards and Makars*, 40 above. For even more on this heroic tale of Bannatyne's labours see Alasdair MacDonald's interesting essay, 'The Bannatyne Manuscript – A Marian Anthology', *Innes Review*, vol. 37, 1986.

E. OTHER AULD MAKARS

Gavin Douglas finished his translation of Virgil's *Aeneid* only a few
weeks before the disastrous defeat of the Scots at Flodden on 9th
September 1513. This has been seen as the day when a curtain came
down on the greatest period of Scots poetry, as well as being the
beginning of what were perhaps the most self-destructive years in
the history of Scotland – and we are not lacking in turbulent
self-destruction in any period of Scotland's history. But poetic
traditions do not die easily, as we can see as I write 476 years after
the death of James IV on Flodden field. However, the middle of the
sixteenth century was a period of lesser achievement by Scottish
poets after the great poetry of the beginning of the century. I think
it is over-easy to put this down to the disaster of Flodden or the
political unrest. Although the English were the victors of Flodden,
their poetry flourished little better. Nevertheless, the poetry of Sir
David Lyndsay, Sir Richard Maitland and Alexander Scott, who are
listed below, shows that all was far from being darkness in Scotland
on the poetry front. There has been a tendency for critics or literary
historians, especially if they are also poets, to exaggerate the decline
of Scottish poetry at various times in Scottish history: Flodden,
Union of Crowns, Reformation, Union of Parliaments, etc., etc. Of
course that is a sad history that worked against an independent
Scottish culture, but poets can survive the most cruel political or
cultural pressures and even be vitalised by such difficult times.
Certainly it is true that the poets of Scotland have over-often lacked
a supporting culture, but let us not under-estimate what brave poets
wrote – and all poets have to be courageous even if only in facing
their own personal fears or 'desert places', to echo Robert Frost.

SIR DAVID LYNDSAY (1486–1555)

158 *The Works of Sir David Lindsay of the Mount 1490–1555*, ed. Douglas
     Hamer, 4 Volumes, Edinburgh, Blackwood for the Scottish Text
     Society, 1931-36.
159 *Poems*, ed. Maurice Lindsay, Edinburgh, Oliver & Boyd for The
     Saltire Society, 1948. The Saltire Classics.
     This is a selection. As its editor writes, 'The merest apéritif to
     sharpen the desire of my countrymen for the full meal'.
     Until Burns, Lyndsay was the poet read by the ordinary people of
     Scotland. Maurice Lindsay has seen him as our first radical poet and
     Walter Scott has a line in *Marmion*, 'the flash of that satiric rage'. I
     regard myself as having a radical stance and as being receptive to
     most kinds of poetry, but somehow I have never responded to

Lyndsay's. However, I have no doubt that he is a poet to swallow in large gulps. My lack of enthusiasm is no doubt a fault in me as those whose judgment I respect tell me I am missing the reality that is in a great poet's work.

Today Lyndsay is best known for his play, *Ane Satyre of the Thrie Estaitis* which, strictly classifying, is outside the remit of this book. According to Hamer, editor of the Scottish Text Society's edition of Lyndsay's work (Volume II), 158 above, the play was performed 'in the Banqueting Hall in the Palace at Linlithgow before James V and Marie de Lorraine, together with the Lords Spiritual and Temporal, at the Feast of the Epiphany, 6th January 1540'. It seems that no text survives of this version, which has been described as an 'Interlude'. An extended version was performed on the Castle Hill, Cupar, Fife, on 7th June 1552. Something of this performance was perhaps preserved in that wonder of wonders, the Bannatyne Manuscript, but I will not venture into this interestingly debatable land of the provenance of these texts[1]. The play was perhaps first printed in what may be a text of a repeat of the Cupar performance which was performed on the Playfield at the Greenside below the Calton Hill in Edinburgh, a performance which has been said to have lasted from 9am till 7pm, no doubt with breaks for refreshment. The publisher was Robert Charteris, the date 1602. The Edinburgh production was performed on Sunday, 12th August 1554, before Marie de Lorraine, Queen-Regent. The next production was on 24th August 1948! This was the celebrated one at the second Edinburgh Festival. Robert Kemp was commissioned by Tyrone Guthrie to create a text of the play suited to the number of hours that a modern audience expected, and he did it superbly well. There have been other productions at other Edinburgh Festivals and elsewhere. The full text was edited by James Kinsley, London, Cassell, 1954, and a modernised acting version was edited by Matthew P. McDiarmid, London, Heinemann, 1967, from Robert Kemp's text first published, Edinburgh, Scots Review, 1949. A new scholarly text by Roderick Lyall, was published in 1989, Edinburgh, Canongate, in the Canongate Classics series.

I catalogue this history of one play, outside my remit, from a courtly setting when Scotland was one of the independent nations of Europe to the excellent scholarly edition of Professor Lyall, to

[1]For fascinating scholarly essays on the early productions of *Ane Satyre* see: John MacQueen, 'Ane Satyre of the Thrie Estaitis', *Studies in Scottish Literature*, vol. 3, no. 3, January 1966; Anna Jean Mill, 'The Original Version of Lindsay's *Satyre of the Thrie Estaitis*', *Studies in Scottish Literature*, vol. 6, no. 2, October, 1968; and Vernon Harward, '*Ane Satyre of the Thrie Estaitis* Again', *Studies in Scottish Literature*, vol. 7, no. 3, January 1970 etc.

show the strength of the Scots tradiiton and the Scots language. Many of that international audience in Edinburgh in 1948 would not have heard Scots spoken before, but what they revealed by their enthusiastic response to the *Satyre* was that any literary art form achieves true communication if its language is authentic.

160 W. Murison, *Sir David Lyndsay: Poet, and Satirist of the Old Church in Scotland*, Cambridge, Cambridge University Press, 1938.

THE GUDE AND GODLIE BALLATIS

161 *A Compendious Book of Godly and Spiritual Songs Commonly Known as 'The Gude and Godlie Ballatis'*, ed. A.F. Mitchell, Edinburgh, Blackwood for the Scottish Text Society, 1897.

162 *The Gude and Godlie Ballatis*, ed. Iain Ross, Edinburgh, Oliver & Boyd for The Saltire Society, 1940. The Saltire Classics.

The history of the publication of these 'sacred songs and ballads' is, like many other works of early Scottish poetry, lost in the books that have not survived. The predecessors of the edition of 1567 which Mitchell used for his Scottish Text Society edition may have been rather less structured works printed in the early 1540s. These *Ballatis* are works of the Reformation which Mitchell saw as not only pulling down the old corrupt pre-Reformation order but building up a world true to all that was sacred and good. They are propaganda and successful in their aims if their popularity can be taken as a guide to that. Why indeed should the devil have all the best songs?

No doubt like all 'folk' songs, to use a term that may be unscholarly but apt nevertheless, they evolved, but it can be said that John Wedderburn was important in giving form to these devotional works, perhaps with the assistance of his brothers James and Robert. Iain Ross's selection is admirably done and perhaps as much as many readers will wish to have.

SIR RICHARD MAITLAND (1496–1586)

163 *The Poems of Sir Richard Maitland of Lethingtoun, Knight*, ed. Joseph Bain, Glasgow, The Maitland Club, 1830. Has an Appendix of selections from the Poems of Sir John Maitland, Lord Thirlestane and of Thomas Maitland. Reprinted New York, AMS Press, 1973. The two poets of the Appendix are Maitland's sons.

As with so many other Scottish poets of quite considerable achievement, Maitland has been overshadowed by a tendency by critics or readers to concentrate on a few great poets. Maitland is a poet of importance within the Scots tradition; not a great poet on the stage of world literature but a poet whose best poems should be read in Scottish schools. In a real sense Maitland's introspective poems make him seem unexpectedly modern. In a way, as Browning can be seen as our man in the nineteenth century, I have a sense in the best of Maitland that within his range he is my man in the sixteenth century. See, for example, 'Solace in Age'.

The wise Moray McLaren writes well of Maitland in his anthology, *The Wisdom of the Scot*, 63 above, and prints five of his poems which give a good general view of both his strengths and weaknesses as a poet. R.D.S. Jack's anthology, 75 above, prints four poems by Maitland. As McLaren admirably says, 'Some of Maitland's verses are dull, but others are memorable for their largemindedness and humanity.' The titles in McLaren's book are a problem but, to take those used by R.D.S Jack, the best of Maitland's poems are, 'Satire on the Age' (the Age being what the Reformation had made of Scotland), 'Solace in Age', 'Aganis the Theivis of Liddisdaill' and one not in Jack, 'The Blind Baronis Comfort'.

This is a wise, old poet. Blind physically, he is not so in his imaginative eye. I like to think of Ronsard writing his poem of calm melancholy to Mary as she left to return to Scotland, and Maitland writing his to welcome his Queen back. He may not have written many poems that we would wish to read today, but they are of a kind rare in Scottish poetry – moderate without being conservative in our modern sense, balanced yet not soft-centred, sensible but not without rage, and rage not without laughing at himself for it.

Maitland cannot be passed without reference to his, and his daughter's, great manuscript collections of Scottish poetry. His Manuscript is important not least for his own poems. He began his about 1570. The Maitland Manuscripts have been edited by William Craigie for the Scottish Text Society; two volumes, 1919 and 1927, being Maitland's own Folio Manuscript, and the 1920 volume being the Quarto of his daughter Marie.

Having previously referred to the Bannatyne Manuscript, I would refer here to another important early manuscript, the Asloan, which was written *c.*1515. It too was edited by Craigie, for the Scottish Text Society, 2 volumes, 1923–5. The two Maitland Manuscripts are held by Magdalene College, Cambridge, in the Pepysian Library; the Bannatyne and Asloan are in The National Library of Scotland.

ALEXANDER SCOTT (*c.*1515–*c.*1583)

164 *The Poems of Alexander Scott*, ed. James Cranstoun, Edinburgh, Blackwood for the Scottish Text Society, 1896.

165 *The Poems of Alexander Scott*, ed. Alexander Karley Donald, London, Kegan Paul, Trench, Trubner for the Early English Text Society, 1902. Reprinted 1973. Extra series no. 85.

166 *The Poems*, ed. Alexander Scott, Edinburgh, Oliver & Boyd for The
     Saltire Society, 1952. The Saltire Classics.
     The simplified spelling was a mistake.
     See also 72 above, *Ballattis of Luve*, ed. John MacQueen, Edinburgh,
     Edinburgh University Press, 1970. This anthology has excellent
     texts of Alexander Scott's love poems and Professor MacQueen's
     Introduction is indispensable for an understanding of Scott's poetry.
167 *Cassette
     Poems*, selected by John MacQueen, Glasgow, Scotsoun, 1978. SSC
     043.

     The modern Alexander Scott writes well on his great namesake's
     poems in his Introduction to 166 above, seeing them as 'Satirical,
     bawdy, elated, fervent, resigned and rebellious in turn, they reflect
     in their variety the extremely various and inextricably entangled
     patterns of love and lust'. In his essay, 'Sixteenth-Century Secular
     Poetry' in 27(a) above, Gregory Kratzmann writes of Scott's 'Up,
     Helsum Hairt' as being memorable for its 'synthesis of high rhetoric
     and simple colloquialism to create the illusion of a speaking voice'.
     So the technique is complicated beyond the metrics. The editor of
     the Scottish Text Society edition gives us almost two pages on
     'Scott as a poet' – it is nineteenth-century nonsense, but worth
     reading for its almost surreal quality. He sees no passion in the
     poetry and writes of this great poet, 'He had little imagination, and
     no great power of pathos and passionate appeal.' This of love poetry
     unmatched in Scottish poetry until Burns, which is not to
     underestimate the achievement of either poet.
168 John MacQueen, *Alexander Scott and Scottish Court Poetry of the
     Middle Sixteenth Century*, Warton Lecture on English Poetry British
     Academy 1968, From the Proceedings of the British Academy, vol.
     54, London, Oxford University Press, 1968.
169 Helena Mennie Shire, *Song, Dance and Poetry of the Court of Scotland
     under King James VI*, Cambridge, Cambridge University Press, 1969.

     In conjunction with Alexander Scott's poems I would refer to a fine
     anonymous poem 'My Hairt is Heich Aboif' which matches him. It
     is in the MacQueen/Scott anthology, 66 above, under 'Anonymous
     (Reigns of James V and Mary I)' as are other good anonymous
     poems, including the hauntingly beautiful eight lines of 'The Reid in
     the Loch Sayis'.

F. LATIN POETRY

Latin is the fourth language of Scottish literature with Gaelic, Scots and English. Latin works have been documented since the sixth century; St Columba wrote hymns in Scotland in the second half of that century. As with all early Scottish poetry, we can assume that much has been lost.

GEORGE BUCHANAN (1506–82)

170 *Opera Omnia*, ed. Thomas Ruddiman, 2 Volumes, Edinburgh, Freebairn, 1715.

George Buchanan is the greatest Scottish Latinist, and in his own time recognised as a major writer throughout Europe. His fame lingers on even amongst Scots who have not read one word that he wrote. His dedication to Queen Mary at the head of his version of the psalms is one of the great short poems of Scottish literature. Leicester Bradner in his book listed below, writes 'surely no poetical tribute to a monarch since the days of Augustus has received so perfect a literary form or been so often quoted'. Equally famous, especially to patriotic Scots, is the passage in his epithalamium addressed to Mary's bridegroom, the Dauphin of France, in which his eloquence reveals the greatness of Scotland and the Scottish people. 'Illa pharatratis est propia gloria Scotis' is the first of fifty-seven lines unsurpassed in Scottish poetry.

The other great Scottish Latinist is Arthur Johnston (1577–1641) who is best known to non-Latinists for his *Apologia piscatoris* ('A Fisherman's Defence'). Hugh MacDiarmid translated this work into English prose, as he did Buchanan's epithalamium as well as his poem on the humanists in Paris. These versions reveal little of the original as poetry. Robert Garioch's 'The Humanists' Trauchles in Paris' is more important (see his *Complete Poetical Works*, 1983, 416 below). Garioch also translated two tragedies by Buchanan – *Baptistes* (on John the Baptist) and *Jephthes* (on the Old Testament story of Jeptha) – see 415 below.

171 Leicester Bradner, *Musae Anglicanae: A History of Anglo-Latin Poetry 1500–1925*, New York, Modern Language Association of America, London, Oxford University Press, 1940.

172 I.D. McFarlane, *Buchanan*, London, Duckworth, 1981.

173 Philip J. Ford, *George Buchanan, Prince of Poets, with an edition (Text, Translation, Commentary) of the 'Miscellaneorum Liber' by Philip J. Ford and W.S. Watt*, Aberdeen, Aberdeen University Press, 1982.

SECTION IV
First Renaissance Poets
(Sixteenth–Seventeenth Centuries)

A. SCOTS POETS

The young King James VI was, as he remained throughout his life, an ambitious man, and not least so with regard to literature. He quite deliberately set out to create a renaissance in Scottish poetry, writing, as a very young man, a manifesto for it in his 'Ane Schort Treatise Conteining Some Reulis and Cautelis to be observit and eshewit in Scottis Poesie'. Like all such programmes for a literary movement it said, as Ezra Pound put it so succinctly – 'Make it New!' And King James, again like Pound, looked to the best of European poetry as a useful guide. In this century, writing his manifesto for a twentieth-century renaissance, Hugh MacDiarmid, like James VI, wished Scottish poetry to be aligned with the latest advances in poetic theory and practice in Europe. James's 'Treatise' reveals the influence of Du Bellay and Ronsard; in MacDiarmid's 'Programme' printed in his magazine *The Scottish Chapbook* in 1922, one of his aims was, 'to bring Scottish Literature into closer touch with current European tendencies in technique and ideation'. King James, having not only his published treatise but a Court, invited European poets to Edinburgh so that Scotland was, in R.D.S. Jack's words, in his anthology 75 above, 'again establishing itself as a centre of European culture, much as it had been in the late fifteenth century'. James's renaissance, as MacDiarmid's, was to be distinctly Scottish, and different from English literature. As James wrote, 'we differ from thame in sindrie reulis of Poesie'. And MacDiarmid in 1922 proclaimed that for a renaissance of Scottish poetry writers had to, 'develop the distinctively Scottish range of values'.

When James VI went off to be King James I of England he developed different literary ambitions which had nothing to do with the Scottish tradition or the Scottish language. But before that sad day in 1603 James had gathered around him the poets of what has been termed his 'Castalian Band'. Among its members was Alexander Montgomerie who had been an established poet in the reign of Mary and he was recognised as 'maister poete' by the Band. Others included were William Fowler (1560–1612) and John Stewart of Baldynneis. King James's own poetry is no great achievement but not unimportant in the context of his renaissance. For full texts of James's poems see *The Poems of King James VI of Scotland*, ed. James Craigie, 2 Volumes, Edinburgh, Blackwood for the Scottish Text Society, 1955–8. Volume I includes 'Some Reulis and Cautelis' which was originally printed in King James's first collection of poetry, *The Essayes of a Prentise in the Divine Art of Poesie*, 1584.

For Fowler's works see *The Works of William Fowler*, eds. Henry W. Meikle, James Craigie and John Purves, 3 Volumes, Edinburgh, Blackwood for the Scottish Text Society, 1914– 40.

R.D.S. Jack's anthology, *A Choice of Scottish Verse 1560–1660*, 75 above, is the best introduction to the poetry of this First Renaissance period, and beyond into the post-Union-of-the-Crowns period. But see also Helena Mennie Shire's most enjoyable – and scholarly – *Song, Dance and Poetry of the Court of Scotland under King James VI*, 169 above. Professor Jack's *The Italian Influence on Scottish Literature*, Edinburgh, Edinburgh University Press, 1972, has a very interesting chapter on 'The Castalian Band'. There is a cassette, *Early Scottish Music*, performed superbly well by Kincorth Waits, Turriff, Heritage Sound, HRT 0010. This is music of the sixteenth and seventeenth centuries and includes settings of poetry by Alexander Montgomerie.

ALEXANDER MONTGOMERIE (*c.*1545–1598)

174 *The Poems of Alexander Montgomerie*, ed. James Cranstoun, Edinburgh, Blackwood for the Scottish Text Society, 1887.

175 *The Poems of Alexander Montgomerie, Supplementary Volume*, ed. George Stevenson, Edinburgh, Blackwood for the Scottish Text Society, 1910.

176 *Alexander Montgomerie. A Selection from His Songs and Poems*, ed. Helena M. Shire, Edinburgh, Oliver & Boyd for The Saltire Society, 1960. The Saltire Classics.

177 *Cassette*
   Alexander Montgomerie. Poems and Songs, selected by Helena M. Shire, Glasgow, Scotsoun, 1981, SSC 060.

Like all leaders of poets, King James VI, being only human, had trouble with members of his Castalian Band, and not least with Alexander Montgomerie who was involved with the Catholic cause, exiled and eventually outlawed. The King seems to have forgiven the poet if not the political or religious activities of Montgomerie. He termed him 'the prince of Poets in our land' and in that he was correct. Like many others of this period, Montgomerie wrote a large number of sonnets, short poems, and songs, including the sonnet 'To

His Mistress' described by Tom Scott in his anthology, 67 above, as 'an involved love-metaphysics'. The 'Lyk as Dum Solsequim' is beautiful in its melancholy. The equally beautiful 'Hay, now the Day Dawis' is a superbly re-cobbled folk song which some see as singable to the tune of 'Scots Wha Hae'. All these poems are in R.D.S. Jack's anthology, 75 above, as is Montgomerie's longer work, 'The Cherrie and the Slae' which is his greatest achievement.

'The Cherrie and the Slae' was an extremely popular poem during the seventeenth and eighteenth centuries. As Cranstoun wrote, 174 above, 'it caught the popular ear at once'. It is a most beautiful poem but complex, although more difficult to nineteenth century readers than to those in the days of its popularity. It is an allegory, the traditional dream-form. Although, seemingly, at one level a love poem rooted in the earlier erotic allegories, it has also been seen to have religious, moral and political significance. Modern critics have tied themselves in knots over it, and very interestingly too. Agnes Mure Mackenzie, unlike many earlier critics, in her essay in Kinsley's *Scottish Poetry*, 38 above, sees not so much allegory but rather what a twenties critic might have termed stream-of-consciousness writing. Professor Jack has written extensively on the poem, and although I believe that he over-emphasises the religious element, he gets it fundamentally right when he sees the poem as charting a 'spiritual progression'.

This progression begins with debate arising out of understandings of love and moves to more complex understandings invoking also analytical and intellectual dialectics. How we see the symbols of cherrie and slae depends, as always of course, upon our individual responses. Moray McLaren writes interestingly of this poem in his anthology, 63 above, and Helena M. Shire, in 169 above, temptingly sees the cherrie as symbolising the Crown of Britain hanging temptingly before James VI of Scotland. Or is the cherrie Catholicism and the slae Protestantism? For R.D.S. Jack's interpretation, see his essay in 27(a) above, and in his book, 178 below, he writes: 'The metaphors employed confirm that this is a universal allegory, able to accommodate particular aims, but striving to be a lesson for all men. In that universality lies the key to its popularity and on that universality critical stress must lie.'

The text of 'The Cherrie and the Slae' in Cranstoun's edition, 174 above, leaves much to be desired and for a good modern text see R.D.S. Jack's anthology, 75 above.

The flyting – abusive verbal and metrical virtuosity – between poets goes back a long way in Scottish poetry. There is *The Flyting of Dunbar and Kennedie* and now we have *The Flyting Betwixt*

Montgomerie and Polwart which may have been written around 1580. It was very popular, being reprinted throughout the seventeenth century. A good extract is printed in *Longer Scottish Poems, Volume I*, 77 above. See Priscilla Bawcutt, 'The Art of Flyting', *Scotttish Literary Journal*, vol. 10, no. 2, December 1983 and Edwin Morgan, 'Flyting' in his *Crossing the Border*, Manchester, Carcanet, 1990 from a lecture, November 1987.

178　R.D.S. Jack, *Alexander Montgomerie*, Edinburgh, Scottish Academic Press, 1985. Scottish Writers series.

JOHN STEWART OF BALDYNNEIS (*c*.1550–*c*.1605)

179　*The Poems of John Stewart of Baldynneis*, ed. Thomas Crockett, Edinburgh, Blackwood for the Scottish Text Society, 1913.

John Stewart is yet another example of a good, although not major, Scottish poet who has been unfairly neglected. That he was neglected was a belief he himself held, at least with regard to his non-poetry life at Court. He was, to intrude into this guide a biographical note of no importance, the son of one of James V's mistresses and his mother was involved in a particularly nasty divorce. The poet went to prison and received no royal preference despite his toadying to the King in his long 'Ane Schersing Out of Trew Felicitie'. But his 'abbregement' of Ariosto's *Orlando Furioso* is another matter altogether, although it was written almost by royal command as a part of James VI's campaign to take Scottish poetry back into the 'mainstream of European poetry', to intrude again a phrase of MacDiarmid's into these royal aims. But it is a translation that lives on the page, particularly the section on Orlando's madness where the strength of Stewart's Scots gives us lines that perhaps exceed the original. Not, of course, that the Scot could have achieved an epic on his own, presumably. But his cutting of the long original is very well done. R.D.S. Jack quotes Matthew P. McDiarmid's opinion of this as 'the most brilliant and energetic poem of the brief Scots Renaissance'. Professor Jack very shrewdly included the section on Orlando's madness in his anthology, 75 above. He also gives us a good selection of sonnets by Stewart.

180　Geoffrey A. Dunlop, 'John Stewart of Baldynneis, the Scottish Desportes', *Scottish Historical Review*, vol. 12, 1915.

181　Matthew P. McDiarmid, 'Notes on the Poems of John Stewart of Baldynneis', *Review of English Studies*, 24, 1948.

182　Timothy G.A. Nelson, 'John Stewart of Baldynneis and *Orlando Furioso*', *Studies in Scottish Literature*, vol. 6, no. 2, October 1968.

ALEXANDER HUME (1557–1609)

183 *The Poems of Alexander Hume*, ed. Alexander Lawson, Edinburgh, Blackwood for the Scottish Text Society, 1902.

A protestant religious poet who in 1597 became minister of the Reformed Church at Logie, near Stirling, Alexander Hume wrote six fine mystical nature poems. In his essay 'A Note on Alexander Hume' in *Scottish Literary News*, vol. 2, nos. 2 and 3, March 1972, Tom Scott indicates the poem 'Of God's Benefites bestowed upon Man' as 'the best mystical poem written by a Scot up to that time, and perhaps ever'. But, like many other critics, Dr Scott sees Hume's 'best achieved' poem as 'Of the Day Estivall'. What a joy is that summer's day. The anthologist of *Longer Scottish Poems, Volume I*, 77 above, refers to the Protestantism of Hume and to the poem having close affinities with the Psalms. She continues, 'the object of describing Nature is to sing "the praise of God"'. This is true, but not finally important to me as I read the poem. Hume rises above any sectarian beliefs to achieve a nature-religious poem that is rooted in a unified yet diverse imaginative reality. In other words, it rises above the individual to express a beauty and a truth that is to be found only in great poetry. But without his sense of religion he would not have achieved this poem which expresses something that is in the poet's inner being.

To Professor Jack 'this poem with its precise and imaginative description of nature is a remarkable phenomenon for the period'. And Alexander Lawson, editor of the Scottish Text Society's edition of Hume's poems, writes most excellently that in 'Of the Day Estivall' Hume is a poet 'whose soul seems to live upon natural sights and sounds'. But the last word on Hume must be with Professor Jack, who indicates some other poems by Hume in his essay in 27(a) above. He writes of 'Of the Day Estivall' that it in particular amongst Hume's work 'reminds us that Presbyterian distrust of mythology, certain types of imagery and aureate language need not always work against art. The poem's power derives first of all from simple, vivid descriptions of the passing phases of the day . . . But the circular form of the poem, beginning and ending with God, also reminds us that every one of these details is valued not in and for itself but as proof that Nature is a statement of divine order and a test of faith through perception.'

MARK ALEXANDER BOYD (1563–1601)

Only one poem in Scots by Boyd – he also wrote in Latin – has come down to us but it is a masterpiece; one of the great sonnets of world literature, 'Fra banc to banc, fra wod to wod, I rin'. In the Petrarchan sonnet form, it ends with genius, 'Led be a blind and teichit be a bairn'.

This famous poem appears in many anthologies.

B. POETRY IN ENGLISH
(SEVENTEENTH CENTURY)

Quite a gaggle of poets followed James VI south to London including Sir William Alexander of Menstrie, later Earl of Stirling (1567–1640), whose poetry was read by the young Milton and praised by Addison. Another poet at the court of James VI in London, and Charles I, was Sir Robert Ayton (1569–1638), a friend of Ben Jonson who did not suffer mini-poets lightly. The young Alexander in Scotland was a late Castalian, as was Ayton, although whether at court or not is uncertain. Ayton was to become a Cavalier poet in London who wrote in English but in his first guise he wrote in Scots. His early Scots poems were to be anglicised for a southern readership with marked loss of vigour as when the nonchalant passer-by, 'the rectles bodie' becomes 'civil person'. See Helena Mennie Shire, *Song, Dance and Poetry of the Court of Scotland Under King James VI*, 169 above, and also M. P. McDiarmid, 'Some Versions of Poems by Sir Robert Aytoun and Sir William Alexander', *Notes and Queries*, n.s. 4, [1957].

R.D.S. Jack includes in his anthology, 75 above, Ayton's 'To His Coy Mistres', which reveals the Scot to be no Marvell, and also five sonnets, the first of which enables us to compare its Scots to the English of the others. This is the poetry of a man of grace, style and wit – and admirable craftsmanship – but, despite Ben Jonson, a lightweight poet. The stay-at-home poets fared little better than the London courtiers. They too attempted, often, an English language. Sir William Mure of Rowallan (1594–1657) is perhaps the best of them. Zachary Boyd (c.1585–1653) is excellently dismissed by Michael Spiller as having the worst ear of his time.

Dr Spiller also writes 'Not a faulty ear, but a stuffed head was the handicap of Alexander Craig' – stuffing being classical learning which he imposed uncreatively on his poetry. Craig (c.1567–1627) went south to publish two volumes of verses and to seek the King's favour. This he did but only briefly and he returned to Scotland where he wrote more poetry and attempted long-distance Castalian favour-seeking from the King – unsuccessfully. He named himself 'Scoto-Brittaine' and in London, as Maurice Lindsay says in his *History of Scottish Literature*, 25 above, Craig revealed, as did many others, 'that all too familiarly unpleasant spectacle, the "Scot-on-the-Make" '. But, taking a further hint from Dr Spiller, I have faced up to the substantial bulk of Craig's poetry and there is indeed, under the mountain of dross, a poet whose words can impart emotion and who deserves 'the tribute of some deft anthologising'.

I take Michael Spiller's advice from his essay in Volume I of *The History of Scottish Literature*, 27(a) above. The task of anthologising these poets has been begun by R.D.S. Jack in his *A Choice of Scottish Verse 1560–1660*, 75 above. Amongst the sonneteers in this anthology are Hugh Barclay (c.1560–1597) and Sir David Murray (1567–1629), another Scoto-Brittaine, and professional courtier. He was latterly principal attendent to Henry, Prince of Wales at the English court but fell out of favour after his master's death. But excellent though it is to find some true poems amongst the dross, the only major poet of this period who wrote in Scoto-English was William Drummond. Before moving on to him I list the editions of the lesser poets.

184 *The Poetical Works of Sir William Alexander, Earl of Stirling* eds. L.E. Kastner and H.B. Charlton, 2 Volumes, Edinburgh, Blackwood for the Scottish Text Society, 1921–29. Volume 1 prints the dramatic works and Volume 2 the non-dramatic works.

185 *The English and Latin Poems of Sir Robert Ayton*, ed. Charles B. Gullans, Edinburgh, Blackwood for the Scottish Text Society, 1963. As Helena Minnie Shire indicates in her *Song, Dance and Poetry of the Court of Scotland Under King James VI*, see 169 above, the unqualified titling of the vernacular poems as 'The English Poems' is 'surprising'.

186 *The Poetical Works of Alexander Craig of Rose-craig*, Glasgow, the Hunterian Club, 1873. The Introduction is by David Laing.

187 *The Works of Sir William Mure of Rowallan*, ed. William Tough, 2 Volumes, Edinburgh, Blackwood for the Scottish Text Society, 1898.

WILLIAM DRUMMOND (1585–1649)

188 *The Poetical Works of William Drummond of Hawthornden*. ed. L.E. Kastner, 2 Volumes, Manchester, Manchester University Press, 1913. Reprinted, Blackwood for the Scottish Text Society, 1913. Also included is the prose piece, 'A Cypresse Grove'.

189 *William Drummond of Hawthornden: Poems and Prose*, ed. Robert H. MacDonald, Edinburgh, Scottish Academic Press, 1976. This is a very good selection with an excellent Introduction by Robert H. MacDonald. More attention should have been, and should be, paid to this book which is the best introduction to Drummond's poetry.

William Drummond was dismissed in the following sentence by

Tom Scott in the Introduction to his Penguin anthology, 67 above: 'William Drummond belongs to the English tradition of poetry, where, for the purposes of this anthology, I am content to leave him.' This I quote to reveal one attitude to Drummond, who has been seen by nationalistic critics as a betrayer of the Scots language by writing in English, which was the language of the Court which had moved from Edinburgh to London, although Drummond remained in Scotland. I for one do believe that he was one of the first poets who did betray their mother tongue, but poetry is not about such matters when read for itself, which is not to say that cultural quislingism should be accepted during the life of a man, or forgiven even centuries later. But the poetry was written and it is important poetry by a Scotsman, like many another who *could* be banished to the English tradition.

Equally Drummond could be evicted altogether from Parnassus Hill for being only a collage of echoes from most of the love poetry of renaissance Europe. But, by that imponderable and illogical force that enables men and women to write poetry, he in fact gives that barrage of echoes a voice that is his own, and perhaps also a particularly Scottish voice. Professor Jack makes an interesting comparison with regard to Drummond's assimilation of so many foreign voices, 'Like Hugh MacDiarmid, the leader of the modern makars, he welcomed all earlier and contemporary literature as material for his poetic inspiration. Yet throughout all this Drummond, no less than MacDiarmid, has a profoundly original viewpoint and voice'.

Some have seen Drummond's poetry as over-cold in its technique and, indeed, overall as the poetry of a man of the library, burning the lamp. Michael Spiller, however, in his essay, 27(a) above, makes what I found to be a rather surprising claim; he sees the poet having 'turned at the close elsewhere than to the poetry of passion, in which, till Burns, he has no native rival'. And yet, ignoring the comparative judgment, he is, when read as a writer of *sequences* rather than anthology-piece poems, indeed a writer of poems of 'passion'. The indication of this *sequential* quality of Drummond's poetry is an important aspect of Robert H. MacDonald's view of the poet. This is important to the way he introduces the poems in the *Poems and Prose* volume, 189 above.

In the first sentence of his selection from the poetry and prose, Robert H. MacDonald writes, 'Drummond of Hawthornden, it could be argued, was the best poet Scotland produced between Douglas and Ramsay.' That is indeed arguable, but perhaps less debatable is MacDonald's next sentence, 'Certainly he ranks higher than any other Scot of the seventeenth century, and looking south, he holds his own as one of the superior craftsmen of his age.' But again, I would reject comparative judgments and turn to a statement about the poetry in its own right.

Edwin Morgan in his essay in *Bards and Makars*, 40 above, and reprinted in Morgan's *Crossing the Border*, 62 above, writes on Gavin Douglas and Drummond as translators, but also gives this admirably projective description of the latter's original poetry, 'Drummond is first and foremost a meditative lyric poet, but he also wrote satirical, political, scabrous, and bawdy verse (some of which, as we now know, was silently omitted by the prudish Kastner from his Scottish Text Society edition). The overall reassessment will have to take all his work into account, and not just the Palgrave's Golden Treasury part of it.' See also in Morgan's *Crossing the Border*, his essay, 'How Good a Poet is Drummond?' reprinted from *Scottish Literary Journal*, vol. 15., no.1, May 1988.

190 David Masson, *Drummond of Hawthornden: The Story of His Life and Writings*, London, Macmillan, 1873.
This remains a very good book, even if, as Robert H. MacDonald says, Masson 'emphasized the romantic poet'.

191 French Rowe Fogle, *A Critical Study of William Drummond of Hawthornden*, New York, Kings Crown Press, Columbia University, 1952.
A good study, but as Professor MacDonald writes, Fogle made 'a sentimental tragedy of the young Scot in love'.
It may be that a poem that is sometimes attributed to Drummond will be omitted from the coming reassessment of him, but I cannot omit it from this book. I refer to the very comic, uproariously funny, macaronic poem, *Polemo-Medinia inter Vitarvam et Nebernam* (or Midden-heid War), or more elaborately, 'The Midden-Fecht between Scotstarvet and Newbarns'. This mock-heroic tale of a Fife village feud is written in what John MacQueen says 'can only be described as joke-Latin', also described elsewhere as dog-Latin or Latin Scots or, as a folio edition of Drummond's works printed by James Watson in 1711 put it, ''Tis a sort of Macaronick poetry in which Scots words are put in Latin Terminations'. Whatever we may term this mixture of Scots and Latin, it is a great joy and a delight. It also, in Professor MacQueen's words, 'demonstrates clearly that poetic composition, despite the Calvinists, need not be divorced from a sense of humour and boisterous fun'. Strangely enough it is not the kirk puritans who object to this mock-heroic tale; it is those who condone every personal licentious act but who protest most vociferously, in the loftiest of literary terms, at spoofs such as this intruding into their own particular puritanical world.

Polemo-Medinia is in Volume II of Kastner's edition, 189 above, where it is categorised as one of the poems that are 'Of Doubtful Authenticity'. The title has become 'Polemo-Middinia'. Quite without rational justification, I am convinced that this is by that reclusive gentleman of more parts than he has been given credit for – William Drummond of Hawthornden. Robert H. MacDonald argues otherwise in 'Amendments to L.E. Kastner's Edition of Drummond's Poems', *Studies in Scottish Literature*, vol. 7, nos. 1 and 2, July–October 1969.

JAMES GRAHAM, MARQUIS OF MONTROSE (1612–50)
Montrose is here because of two verses of perfection from his love poem, a famous anthology piece, with its first line, 'My dear and only love, I pray', and the famous first line of the second stanza, 'As Alexander I will reign'. To that we can add his eight-line 'Prayer' written the night before he mounted his thirty-foot scaffold. So truly he has this separate entry because of the romance of his life. It is surprising to remember that he died in the year after William Drummond who seems almost to be of our modern world. As Agnes Mure Mackenzie movingly says in her essay in Kinsley's *Scottish Poetry*, 38 above, 'The courtly tradition in verse, the accomplishment of the soldier-courtier-scholar, died the year after Drummond, on a dark May day at Edinburgh Cross, when Montrose swung there in three fathoms of rope'.

C. GAELIC POETS (SEVENTEENTH CENTURY)

In her essay in Kinsley's *Scottish Poetry*, 38 above, Agnes Mure Mackenzie, in acknowledging the Gaelic areas of Scotland, wrote 'the stately tradition of bardic verse in Gaelic, hardening out of creativeness by 1500 but reviving by the end of the century in the *dolce stil nuovo* of Mary MacLeod (*c*.1615–1707) and the steel-pointed satire of Charles II's Gaelic Laureate, John Macdonald. Indeed, for much of the seventeenth and eighteenth centuries Gaelic was from the artistic point of view the most important language of the country.'

John MacQueen, in a perceptive section on the Gaelic poets in his *Progress and Poetry*, 18 above, suggests that although Gaelic bardic poetry in the seventeenth century was 'intensely traditional' and so confined largely to 'linked genres of panegyric, satire and elegy', it was at the same time 'of the present, of individual events as they imposed upon a society whose institutions had been stable for a long time'. Professor MacQueen sees the poetry of Mary MacLeod or Iain Lom as revealing a confidence in the 'permanence, as well as the excellence, of the old order, even as it was visibly crumbling before their eyes'. The Lowland poets, such as William Drummond, had no such confidence in the old order of Lowland Scotland. They had recognised the transference of power that had taken place when the Court of *their* King went south to London. Drummond spoke Scots, but he did not believe in Scots as a language of poetry. Culloden would come to undermine Gaelic society, and cultural confidence, but that is almost fifty years after the deaths of Iain Lom and Mary MacLeod, whose work has to be seen in the light of Dr Mackenzie's and Professor MacQueen's statements as being still rooted in an utter confidence in their native language and literary tradition. The work of Sileas MacDonald shows a similar confident stance.

IAIN LOM (JOHN MACDONALD) (*c.*1624–*c.*1707)

192 *Orain Iain Luim. Songs of John MacDonald, Bard of Keppoch,* ed. Annie M. MacKenzie, Edinburgh, Oliver & Boyd for the Scottish Gaelic Texts Society, 1964. Reprinted by Scottish Academic Press for the Society, 1973.

Derick Thomson, in his *An Introduction to Gaelic Poetry,* 39 above, sees the adjective *lom* applied to MacDonald because of his 'gift for the cutting, scathing phrase'. Iain Lom also shows great economy in his use of language, to powerful effect. The editor of his *Songs,* Annie M. MacKenzie, writes in her Introduction, 'His verses reflect the turmoil of the times and also the bitterness of the political struggle and the clan quarrels which took place in his own day. He himself was involved in many of the events which he records and therefore they have a personal interest for him – hence the strong element of personal emotion which characterises his compositions. His name still survives in the traditions of the Highlands as the poet of repartee and satire, and his works undoubtedly constitute the most important source of information in Gaelic for the political scene in seventeenth-century Scotland.' This is a poetry which seems to me, for all its setting in past historical and political events and in the bardic and clan system, to be very modern. I would refer to his great poem, 'Là Inbhir Lochaidh' on the Battle of Inverlochy, which is powerful in its realistic descriptions and its taut yet rich language.

MAIRI NIGHEAN ALASDAIR RUAIDH (MARY MACLEOD) (*c.*1615–1705)

193 *Gaelic Songs,* ed. J.Carmichael Watson, Edinburgh, Scottish Academic Press for the Scottish Gaelic Texts Society, 3rd impression 1983.

First edition, Blackie, 1934.

Mary MacLeod's editor, J. Carmichael Watson, sees the flow of her poetry as 'perfectly spontaneous, natural and effortless' and he ends by quoting Kenneth MacLeod, 'The Gael in his high mood thinks of Deirdre for beauty, Bride for goodness and Mary MacLeod for song'. Derick Thomson writes, in his *An Introduction to Gaelic Poetry*, 39 above, 'What her poetry has *par excellence* is music and rhythm . . .'

SILEAS NA CEAPAICH (SILEAS MACDONALD) (*c.*1660–*c.*1729)

194 *Bàrdachd Shìlis na Ceapaich. Poems and Songs*, ed. Colm Ó Baoill, Edinburgh, Scottish Academic Press for the Scottish Gaelic Texts Society, 1972.

In his *An Introduction to Gaelic Poetry*, 39 above, Derick Thomson reveals Sileas to be a poet of a fairly wide range of forms and subject matter: political poems, what Professor Thomson terms 'a some what more subdued clan interest', a moral stance and a religious one. She works in the folk style but also in the tradition of formal laments. Such a descripton of what her poems are about perhaps gives a grander position to her work than the actual poetry merits. But Professor Thomson uses a most apt phrase when he refers to her ability to 'conduct sinuous poetical argument'. He indicates her poem 'Do dh'Arm Rìgh Sheumais' ('To King James's Army'), probably written in 1715 and certainly after the collapse of the Jacobite campaign, as being probably 'the best example of her sinuous, colourful, figurative style of argument'. Again the strength of the old Gaelic poetic tradition impresses a Lowlander such as myself. The poets, or bards, truly had an importance in their society, and if traditional forms can impose themselves over-powerfully they can, as always, be the base from which an individual poet can move to develop the tradition. Whether this applies to Sileas's work is not something I am qualified to judge, although I suspect that she was content to work within the established parameters of the tradition, and that was doubtless part of her strength. Professor Thomson indicates this confidence, within the Gaelic tradition, which is in the work of the other greater Gaelic poets I have listed in this section, when he writes, 'One can sense her secure, cultured background, and see the evidence of a long literary tradition behind her work'.

SECTION V
Ballads

We use the word ballad variously. There are, to look back a long way, the heroic Gaelic ballads for which I would refer readers to *Leabhar na Féinne*, 64 above, and to the two anthologies of *The Book of the Dean of Lismore*, 69 and 70 above. The Ossianic ballads of the heroic tradition probably go back to around AD 1100, suggests Derick Thomson in his *An Introduction to Gaelic Poetry*, 39 above. These heroic ballads were to some extent what James Macpherson drew on for his European-shattering writings. He may not have truly known the Ossianic ballads or sagas, and may have faked what he did know, but with his half-knowledge of the Gaelic tradition he shifted the creative perspective of Europe.

In addition to these heroic ballads in Gaelic there is another kind of ballad in Gaelic poetry and song. I refer to the popular poem-songs of the sixteenth, seventeenth and eighteenth centuries. Some of this popular oral tradition has been collected in *An t-Oranaiche*, edited by G. Mac-na-Ceàrdadh, Glasgow, Celtic Press, c.1876, and in *The MacDonald Collection of Gaelic Poetry*, eds. A. MacDonald and A. MacDonald, Inverness, The Northern Counties Newspaper Printing and Publishing Co., 1911. Sorley MacLean, in his essay 'Realism in Gaelic Poetry', in 57 above, writes of this song poetry, 'This poetry has a counterpart in the Lowland Scots ballad, but in bulk, range and quality the anonymous Gaelic poetry is immeasurably superior to the Lowland ballads, which sometimes do contain splendid poetry'.

This section is concerned with that 'splendid poetry', but before moving on to details of it I would refer back to James Macpherson. Born in 1736, Macpherson died in 1796 – the same year as Robert Burns. Macpherson was entombed in Westminster Abbey; Burns died in debt. We know now who has the last laugh at that recognition by the establishment. One of the reasons why Burns achieved such popular fame was that he drew authentically on the Lowland popular, or folk, tradition; and so he is linked to the ballads of this section. The Scottish tradition in poetry is, indeed, a seamless garment of popular art and high art in both Gaelic and Scots.

49

195 *Ancient and Modern Scottish Songs, Heroic Ballads, etc.,* ed. [David Herd], 2 Volumes, Edinburgh, 2nd edition, 1776. Various editions, the most recent, 2 Volumes, Edinburgh, Scottish Academic Press, 1973.

196 *Minstrelsy of the Scottish Border,* 2 Volumes, Kelso, James Ballantyne for T. Cadell, Jun. and W. Davies, London, 1802. Second edition, 3 Volumes, Edinburgh, James Ballantyne for Longman & Rees, London, 1803.

The dedication of the first edition is signed by Walter Scott who collected, edited and revised these 'Historical and Romantic Ballads' and supplied a 'few of modern date founded upon local tradition'. There are many later editions, revised and edited, see, T.F. Henderson, 4 Volumes, Edinburgh, Oliver & Boyd, 1932, this edition being originally published in 1902.

197 *Andrew Crawfurd's Collection of Ballads and Songs,* ed. E.B. Lyle, Edinburgh, The Scottish Text Society, Volume I, 1975.

198 *The English and Scottish Popular Ballads,* ed. Francis James Child, 5 Volumes, Boston, Houghton, Mifflin & Company, 1882–98. Reprinted, various editions, see, 5 Volumes, New York, Dover Publications, 1965; this is an unabridged and unaltered republication of the original 1882–98 work.

199 *The Traditional Tunes of the Child Ballads, With their Texts,* ed. Bertrand H. Bronson, Princeton, Princeton University, 4 Volumes, 1959–72.

To indicate where the modern printing or collecting of the ballads or of folk songs begins is a futile task but four names have to be mentioned with regard to Scotsmen: Allan Ramsay, for his *Tea-Table Miscellany*: David Herd, 195 above, who, unlike Ramsay, gave us texts as he found them without cobbling; Sir Walter Scott, whose *Minstrelsy*, 196 above, is of major importance; and Andrew Crawfurd (1786–1854), who left a vast quantity of folk material in manuscript.

The definitive collection of the ballads is by Child, 198 above. The great ballads are now often referred to by the numbers that this major collector and editor gave to them. The great companion work to Child's is Bronson's, 199 above. With these two great works we have both words and tunes; serious study of the ballads begins with them.

200 *Border Ballads,* ed. William Beattie, Harmondsworth, Penguin, 1952. A selection.

201 *The Oxford Book of Ballads,* ed. James Kinsley, Oxford, Clarendon Press, 1969. Paperback edition, 1982. Reprinted. A general selection.

202 *A Scottish Ballad Book*, ed. David Buchan, London, Routledge & Kegan Paul, 1972.
A selection from Northeast tradition.
The great collectors of the ballads in the eighteenth and nineteenth centuries gave us a heritage that is now available in print, but in recent years we have been uniquely privileged to have the ballads available to us on discs and cassettes. This is a restoration of them to their true oral tradition. I therefore give below an extensive discography which I believe to be now at the core of an understanding of the great and classic ballads.

For one great recorded introduction to these ballads I recommend the LPs entitled *The Muckle Sangs: Classic Scots Ballads*, 209 below. These recordings come from the archives of the School of Scottish Studies of Edinburgh University and are introduced with impeccable scholarship by Hamish Henderson in an indispensable 24-page booklet that accompanies the discs. I have elsewhere referred to Hamish Henderson as the 'inspirational heart of the School of Scottish Studies'. On the sleeve of these discs Mr Henderson quotes, as he has done elsewhere, the following ringing sentences by the great Bertrand H. Bronson, which were first printed in *California Folklore Quarterly*, vol. 4, no. 2, 1945: 'Eighteenth-century Scotland, there is no doubt at all, was a nation of ballad singers and ballad lovers. How much earlier it had been so no one knows; but it is a fact that what we today know as British balladry at its best is a mass of texts taken down by interested persons from living Scottish tradition in the latter half of the eighteenth century, or learned then and transmitted to print or manuscript early in the following century.'

DISCOGRAPHY (including cassettes)
For the following list I have drawn on Hamish Henderson's most valuable discographies in *Tocher* from no. 25, Spring 1977, onwards. See also the 'Further Listening' list on the booklet accompanying 209 below, and Hamish Henderson's 'Scots Ballad and Folk Song Recordings', *Scottish Literary News*, vol. 1, no. 2, January 1971. *Tocher* is sub-titled *Tales, Songs, Tradition* and what it prints is selected from the archives of the School of Scottish Studies, Edinburgh University. *Tocher*, ed. Alan Bruford, is published by the School. See also the scholarly journal of the School, *Scottish Studies*, 105 above.

203 *Columbia Albums of Folk and Primitive Music, Volume 6 (Scotland)*, 1953, SL209.
Edited by Alan Lomax this remains, writes Hamish Henderson, 'a stimulating and by no means unrepresentative 'sampler' of one of

the richest and most variegated folk music traditions in Western Europe'. Side 1 is Lowland song and Side 2 Gaelic song. This disc includes the classic ballad 'Glenlogie' (Child 238) sung by John Strachan, and Ewan MacColl's 'virtuoso' performance of 'Dowie Dens o' Yarrow' (Child 214).

204   *The Folk Songs of Britain, Volume 4, The Child Ballads I,* Topic, 1963, 12T 160. Originally New York, Caedmon, 1961.

205   *The Folk Songs of Britain, Volume 5, The Child Ballads II,* Topic, 1963, 12T 161. Originally New York, Caedmon, 1961.

There are eight other LPs in this series which has been described as 'the most stimulating and thought-provoking 'aural' contribution to British folk-song studies ever made'.

The contribution of the traveller singers of the Northeast of Scotland alone makes these records important. The most famous is Jeannie Robertson, discovered by Hamish Henderson, as were many other of the singers, and her rendition of the great ballads is a major contribution to these records. Among items recorded by her on these discs are 'Mary Hamilton' (Child 173), 'Willie's Fate' (Child 225), 'The Jolly Beggar' (Child 279), 'Lord Randal' (Child 12), 'Son David' (Child 13) and 'Young Beichan' (Child 53).

Other Scots singers on these discs are John Strachan, Lucy Stewart, Duncan Burke, Jessie Murray, Davy Stewart, John Stickle, John Sinclair and Ethel Findlater.

JEANNIE ROBERTSON

206   *Great Traditional Singers, No. 1,* Topic 12T 96.

This was originally numbered 12T 52 and issued in 1956, but was reissued under the above no. in 1965. A very useful leaflet is inserted. An earlier version of this LP had appeared in the USA (Riverside) under the title *Songs of a Scots Tinker Lady* which the singer found embarrassing, and she may may well have felt likewise about the guitar accompaniment by Josh Macrae to some of the songs. But Riverside was the first record company to offer Jeannie Robertson a contract. Hamish Henderson describes in *Tocher,* no. 28, 1978, the British version, which has no guitar accompaniments, as 'probably the best single 'sampler' of Jeannie's extraordinary power, virtuosity and glamourie'. It includes 'The Gypsy Laddie' (Child 200) and 'Lord Lovat' (Child 75).

Jeannie Robertson's celebrated version of 'The Battle of Harlaw' (Child 163) is on the first folksong disc issued by the School of Scottish Studies, *Gaelic and Scots Folk Songs* A0003/4. Published in a limited edition of 100 copies in 1960, these songs are from the archives of the School. This disc, like many others that I list, is now a collector's item.

207 *Scottish Ballads and Folk Songs*, 1960, Prestige-International 13006. This includes two of the most famous of her versions of classic ballads, 'Johnnie the Brime' (Child 114) and her world-famous version of 'Edward, Son David' (Child 13).

The American company gave to this LP the not unjustified title *Jeannie Robertson, the World's Greatest Folksinger*.

For further details of recordings by Jeannie Robertson see, Hamish Henderson, 'Scots Folk-song Discography, Part 3', *Tocher*, no. 28, Summer-Spring 1978.

208 *Lucy Stewart, Traditional Singer from Aberdeenshire, Volume I, Child Ballads*, Folkways FG 3519.

The ballads on this album include 'The Battle of Harlaw' (Child 163), 'The Laird o Drum' (Child 236), 'The Bonnie Hoose o Airlie' (Child 199) and 'Barbara Allen' (Child 84).

209 *The Muckle Sangs: Classic Scots Ballads*, Scottish Tradition Volume 5, 1975, Tangent, TNGM 119/D, 2 discs.

Recorded and documented by the School of Scottish Studies, University of Edinburgh.

These two discs are also on one cassette, TNG MMD 119.

These are classic LPs and those that I recommend above. I must reiterate that the scholarship of the insert and sleeve notes is impeccable and most informative. Selection, documentation and text transcripts by Hamish Henderson and Ailie Munro. General commentary by Hamish Henderson, incorporating music commentary by Ailie Munro.

The singers are John Adams, Jeannie Robertson, John MacDonald, Bella Higgins, Duncan Macphee, Nellie MacGregor, Minnie Haman, Sheila MacGregor, Betsy Johnston, Willie Whyte, Lizzie Higgins, Geordie Robertson, Betsy Whyte, Jessie Murray, Willie Edward, Campbell MacLean, Jimmy MacBeath, John Strachan, Margaret Stewart, Willie Scott and Jane Turriff.

Major contents are: 'Glenlogie' (Child 238), 'The Gypsy Laddies' (Child 200), 'The False Knight upon the Road' (Child 3), 'The Bonnie Banks o' Fordie' (Child 14), 'The Twa Brothers' (Child 49), 'Tam Lin' (Child 39), 'The Knight and the Shepherd's Daughter' (Child 110), 'The Bold Pedlar' (Child 132), 'The Twa Sisters' (Child 10), 'The Jolly Beggar' (Child 279 – Appendix), 'Lord Thomas and Fair Ellen' (Child 73), 'Young Johnston' (Child 88), 'Young Beicham (Lord Bateman)' (Child 53), 'The Keach in the Creel' (Child 281), 'Clyde's Water' (Child 216), 'Sir Hugh and the Jew's Daughter' (Child 155), 'Jamie Telfer o' the Fair Dodhead' (Child 190) and 'Andrew Lammie' (Child 233).

I write 'major contents' above to insert some words on Side 1, Band 2b, 'The Roving Ploughboy' sung by John MacDonald. Hamish Henderson identifies the first part of the song as a 'displaced fragment of a version of "Gypsy Laddies" (Child 200)'. The remaining two verses he identifies as having been added locally in the Northeast in recent times, including lines by the singer John MacDonald. And then Jeannie Robertson heard this version of MacDonald's song and was interested in its tune. She set a long version of the Child ballad from which she recognised the song had sprung, and which she had got, writes Henderson, 'orally from her folk to the 'Ploughboy' tune. – It only remains for somebody to use her re-created "Gypsy Laddies" as the starting point for a new lyric song, and the wheel will have come full circle.' I give the above as an example of progressions within the oral folk tradition, but of course the folksongs, which includes the great ballads, can feed into art-poetry.

In writing of 'Tam Lin' in the inserted booklet to these LPs, Hamish Henderson illustrates this at the highest level of such poetry. His recording of the ballad is by Betsy Johnston, is a tale to be told, as he indeed tells it, but he writes, ' "Tam Lin", on the lips of this stravaigin singer, provided instant evidence that the ballad had been travelling around for centuries in the care of these nomadic Johnstons, who were living out elemental ballad themes in South-west Scotland long before Robert Burns was born. In addition, Betsy's version seemed to put into perspective the magnificent 'Tam Lin' which Burns sent to James Johnston for inclusion in *The Scots Musical Museum* – a version which is still (with Lord Hailes's *Edward* and a handful of others) one of the most famous ballad texts in the world. Burns drew on orally transmitted variants from the Borders and the South-West, but he tightened up the narrative and turned the ballad into a poem which reads superbly well on the printed page. In so doing he appears simultaneously as a great art-poet, an eighteenth century-style collector, and a "folk poet writ large".' See also Emily B. Lyle, 'The Burns Text of "Tam Lin" ', *Scottish Studies*, vol. 15, 1971, and for a more general work on Burns and the oral tradition see, Mary Ellen Brown, *Burns and Tradition*, London, Macmillan, 1984.

I give the above details to reveal the curly snake of poetry twisting in on itself. But if the art-poets draw on the folk-songs it is a remarkable fact of Scottish culture that the folk singers draw on art-poetry more than is perhaps customary in other cultures. Hamish Henderson indicates this by quoting Alan Lomax who wrote in 1952, 'what most impressed me was the vigour of the Scots folk-song tradition, on the one hand, and its close connection with the literary sources on the other . . . the Scots have the liveliest folk tradition of the British Isles, but paradoxically, it is the most bookish'.

210 *Jean Redpath's Scottish Ballad Book*, USA, Elektra, EKL 214.
Hamish Henderson describes this early LP as 'a truly fabulous disk which includes recordings of "Barbara Allen", "Tam Lin" and "Clerk Saunders"'.

211 *Jean Redpath: Frae My Ain Countrie*, Folk-legacy, FSS 49. Includes 'breathtaking performances' of 'Kilbogie' (a version of 'Glasgow Peggie') (Child 228) and 'Johnnie O'Breadisley' (Child 114).

212 *Jean Redpath*, Philo, 2015.
Hamish Henderson writes, 'the record notable for her performance of "Lady Dysie", Child 269 – a superb blend of art and scholarship. (She used a printed melody found in Bronson, and fused it with a powerful text collated by herself.)'

213 *Belle Stewart: Queen Among the Heather*, Topic, 12TS 307.
Includes versions of 'The Twa Brothers' (Child 49) and 'Leezie Lindsay' (Child 226).

214 *Isla St Clair Sings Traditional Scottish Songs*, Tangent, 1972, TGS 112.
Includes 'Annie of Lochroyan' which is a version of 'The Lass of Roch Royal' (Child 76).

215 *Alison McMorland: Belt wi Colours Three*, Tangent, 1977, TGS 125.
Includes 'The Swan Swims Sae Bonny O' which is a version of 'The Twa Sisters' (Child 10).
Hamish Henderson writes in *Tocher*, no. 30, Winter 1978–79, 'Alison's art is a marvellous blend of inherited tradition and devoted research'.

216 *Cassette*
Ten Scottish Ballads, Glasgow, Scotsoun, SSC 073.

217 Hamish Henderson and Fr•ncis Collinson, 'New Child Ballad Variants from Oral Tradition', *Scottish Studies*, vol. 9, 1965.

218 Willa Muir, *Living with Ballads*, London, Hogarth Press, 1965.

219 Herschel Gower, 'Jeannie Robertson: Portrait of a Traditional Singer', *Scottish Studies*, vol. 12, 1968.

220 Herschel Gower and James Porter, 'Jeannie Robertson: The Child Ballads', *Scottish Studies*, vol. 14, 1970.
Analyses ten ballads as sung by Jeannie Robertson and gives full transcripts.

221 Ailie Munro, 'Lizzie Higgins and the Oral Transmission of Ten Child Ballads', *Scottish Studies*, vol. 14, 1970.
Lizzie Higgins is a daughter of Jeannie Robertson.

222 Herschel Gower and James Porter, 'Jeannie Robertson: The "Other

Ballads"', *Scottish Studies*, vol. 16, 1972.
An analysis of ten 'non-Child ballads' as sung by Jeannie Robertson.

223 David Buchan, *The Ballad and the Folk*, London, Routledge & Kegan Paul, 1972.
This is the companion volume to Professor Buchan's 202 above. A major work.

224 David Murison, 'The Language of the Ballads', *Scottish Literary Journal*, supplement no. 6 (Language), Spring 1978.

225 *The People's Past*, ed. Edward J. Cowan, Edinburgh, Polygon Books, 1980.

226 James Reed, *Border Ballads*, London, Athlone Press, 1980.

For other essays on the ballads see Sir James Fergusson's in 38 above and Hamish Henderson's in 27(a) above.

SECTION VI
Eighteenth-Century Poets

A. EIGHTEENTH-CENTURY SCOTS RENAISSANCE POETS

The traditional (perhaps scholarly) tendency has been to term the poetry of Allan Ramsay, Robert Fergusson and Robert Burns as the major work of a 'revival' of Scots, or as the 'vernacular revival'. But if the poets of James VI's Castalian Band produced work that constitutes a renaissance of Scottish poetry, then so also, and perhaps even more so, the work of Allan Ramsay, Robert Fergusson and Robert Burns constitutes both revival and renaissance. Of course the word 'renaissance' is pompous and invites writers to preface it with words like 'so-called', but editorial or historical headings or divisions are, finally, all nonsense with regard to what was the living world when the poetry was written.

Before moving to Allan Ramsay's work, I would first look back to the seventeenth-century poet, Robert Sempill of Beltrees (?1595–1665) who was the author of the famous poem, 'The Life and Death of the Piper of Kilbarchan', perhaps better known as 'The Epitaph of Habbie Simson'. Compared with the work of the auld makars this can be seen as a work of lesser standing – in David Daiches' phrase, 'sprightly popular verse'. But that sort of verse was being written also in the time of the great makars and the Scots tradition has always had cross fertilisation of popular and high art in poetry. Although Sempill in his poem did not achieve high art-poetry he, by synthesising high and low, or heich and laich, did give the Scots tradition a form that enabled greater poets to do so. The mock elegy on men and beasts became one of the popular forms of the eighteenth-century renaissance in the work of Ramsay, Fergusson and Burns, the last-named raising it to the level of genius. For a scholarly essay on 'Habbie Simson' see Kenneth Buthlay's in *Bards and Makars*, 40 above.

I would mention also William Hamilton of Gilbertfield (c.1665–1751) who lived as a country gentleman near Cambuslang. He carried on a verse correspondence with Allan Ramsay and his 'Last Dying Words of Bonnie

Heck' continued the 'Habbie Simson' tradition. But unlike the original of Sempill this is a *mock* elegy – and an elegy for an animal; and so the link is made to Robert Burns and to his 'The Death and Dying Words of Poor Mailie'. Ramsay named this verse form 'Standart Habby' in a verse epistle to Hamilton of Gibertfield dated 10th July 1719. Perhaps Ramsay's best poem in the form is 'Elegy on Lucky Wood in the Canongate, May 1717'. There is a further link between Burns and Ramsay in that the former raised the verse correspondence form to the level of great poetry. James Watson included Sempill's 'Habbie Simson' in his important pioneering anthology, *A Choice Collection of Comic and Serious Scots Poems both Ancient and Modern*, which appeared in three parts between 1706 and 1711. These volumes instigated the eighteenth-century renaissance of Scots poetry. The Scottish Text Society published the first volume of an edition of Watson's *Choice Collection* in 1977 edited by Harriet Harvey Wood which is a facsimile of the Glasgow edition of 1869. A second volume of what should be very helpful notes and commentary is due soon.

ALLAN RAMSAY (1684–1758)

227 *The Works of Allan Ramsay*, Volumes I and II eds. Burns Martin and John W. Oliver, Volumes III–VI eds. Alexander M. Kinghorn and Alexander Law, Edinburgh, Blackwood for the Scottish Text Society, 1945–74.

The 'Biographical and Critical Introduction' to Volume IV by Alexander M. Kinghorn gave a new standing to biography and criticism of Ramsay. Volume V, which contains amongst much else 'The Journal of the Easy Club', was undertaken by Dr Law who was living in Ramsay's 'Senex Fumosus' as he facetiously called his adopted city, see also 232 below. This is another major additon to scholarly studies of Scottish literature, giving us new understandings of Ramsay and his time.

228 *Poems by Allan Ramsay and Robert Fergusson*, eds. Alexander Manson Kinghorn and Alexander Law, Edinburgh, Scottish Academic Press for the Association for Scottish Literary Studies, 1974. Paperback edition 1985, in the Scottish Classics series.

A first-rate book through which to approach Ramsay's work as, in addition to the poems, it prints his play *The Gentle Shepherd* extracts from which can be heard on a cassette edited by Alexander Law, Glasgow, Scotsoun, 1979, SSC 052.

229 *Poems: Epistles, Fables, Satires, Elegies & Lyrics*, ed. H. Harvey Wood, Edinburgh, Oliver & Boyd for The Saltire Society, 1946. The Saltire Classics.

The title on the jacket is 'Selected Poems' and a very good selection it is, but it is not the book I would recommend for even a first reading of Ramsay's poems as he is not an extending poet and can be read at length very easily.

230 *Cassette*

Allan Ramsay: Poems and Songs, ed. Alexander Law, Glasgow, Scotsoun, 1979, SSC 051.

If James Watson instigated this eighteenth-century renaissance, then Allan Ramsay gave it its foundations. First of all he established a name as a poet, publishing his poems and songs singly or in small groups. In 1721 he collected his poems and this subscribed edition made him the most famous poet of Edinburgh. His best-selling drama, *The Gentle Shepherd*, was published in 1725. But during the previous year he had begun to continue and expand the publishing activities of Watson with his pioneering *The Ever Green, Being a Collection of Scots Poems, Wrote by the Ingenious before 1600*, (2 Volumes, 1724). This anthology gave his contemporaries texts of the auld makars, including Henryson, Dunbar and Alexander Scott, plus other important poems from the Bannatyne Manuscript. His *Tea-Table Miscellany* was issued in four little volumes between 1723 and 1737. In this anthology Ramsay printed a variety of songs and ballads; some old songs printed as he found them, some revised or 'improved', some imitation folk songs and ballads, some new songs to old tunes. Ramsay said in a later edition that he made verses for 'about sixty of them' and 'about thirty more were done by some ingenious young men'. The success of this *Tea-Table Miscellany* prompted others to publish collections, including David Herd with his *Ancient and Modern Scottish Songs*, 195 above. Unlike Ramsay, Herd did not tamper with what he found and so gave Robert Burns a rich storehouse on which to draw to create new songs and poems that are the masterpieces we know. We blame Ramsay for 'improving' because the end result is often bad, but praise Burns because he rewrote most thoroughly and so gave us poems and songs that revealed his genius. But Ramsay paved the way for Burns and for Robert Fergusson and saved much that might have been lost – and the originals may have been worse than Ramsay's versions!

In terms of world poetry, no-one could call Allan Ramsay a great poet, but he was the greatest Scottish poet of his time, and is a major figure in the Scots tradition. He wrote poems that remain very enjoyable. He is enthusiastic and very much of the convivial popular Scots tradition that, it should not be forgotten, goes back to its beginnings. Of course in Ramsay's time we lack the involvement with the poetry of Europe that we find in Dunbar or Henryson, not that Ramsay does not attempt to be part of a culture that takes in

Greek and Latin even if the poetry is not sufficiently high to realise his aims. As an editor and general activist and enthusiast for Scottish culture, Ramsay is, in his own way, as much an instigator of a renaissance in Scottish poetry as was James VI, and Hugh MacDiarmid in this century. What a trio! In this context Ramsay is a giant. As H. Harvey Wood wrote in his Saltire selection, no. 229 above, 'it may be doubted if any Scotsman ever served the best interests of his country more faithfully than Allan Ramsay'. And Alexander Kinghorn and Alexander Law, in their essay in 27(b) above, write of Ramsay, 'Without him literature in Scotland would have taken a different road. He ensured that the native Muse would survive and flourish.' In his essay in Volume IV of 227 above, Professor Kinghorn writes most admirably, 'when he tried out his Scots, Ramsay had no peer in his own time. Fergusson and Burns excepted, no "Scots Poet" has been more deserving of the title.'

231   Allan H. MacLaine, *Allan Ramsay*, Boston, Twayne Publishers, 1985. English Authors series.

232   Alexander Law, 'Allan Ramsay and the Easy Club', *Scottish Literary Journal*, vol. 16, no. 2, November 1989.

ALEXANDER ROSS (1699–1784)

233   *The Scottish Works of Alexander Ross*, ed. Margaret Wattie, Edinburgh, Blackwood for the Scottish Text Society, 1938.

Alexander Ross was a native of Aberdeenshire and for many years schoolmaster of Lochlee in Angus. He was popular in his lifetime, mainly in his native North-east. In recent times, however, he has been unjustly neglected and when recognised at all it has been for a few songs such as 'The Rock and the Wee Pickle Tow', 'The Bridal O't' and perhaps especially for the truly admirable 'Wooed and Married and A"; the last-named is the only poem by Ross in the MacQueen/Scott anthology, 66 above. There are many other songs of this period which are equally good and two particularly worthy of mention are: John Skinner's 'Tullochgorum' (to Burns 'The best Scotch song Scotland ever saw'), and Jean Elliot's version of 'The Flowers of the Forest'. Of course there is also much anonymous work of this period, as Thomas Crawford's anthology, *Love, Labour and Liberty*, 80 above, admirably reveals. Mr Crawford prints Ross's 'Wooed and Married and A".

However, I list Ross here separately not for his songs but for *The Fortunate Shepherdess: A Pastoral Tale in Three Cantos in the Scottish Dialect*, published in 1768. Later the poem was titled, *Helenore, or the Fortunate Shepherdess*, or even more informally on Ross's tombstone, erected in 1843, where he is described as 'Author of "Lindy and

Nory" or the Fortunate Shepherdess and other poems in the Scottish Dialect'.

This is, of course, the cringe factor imposed upon worthy poets and it makes it difficult for their poetry to be taken seriously. Ross's long poem may not be a major work within the Scots tradition, and may be a lesser work than Allan Ramsay's play, *The Gentle Shepherd*, from which Ross took the germ of his poem, but nevertheless it is important in the context of Scots poetry and has been unduly neglected.

The editors of *Longer Scottish Poems, Volume II*, 81 above, print a good extract from Ross's *Helenore* and make an appeal for a better appreciation of the poem. The Association for Scottish Literary Studies plans to print a new edition of *Helenore*.

234 David Hewitt, 'The Ballad World and Alexander Ross', in *Literature of the North*, eds. David Hewitt and Michael Spiller, Aberdeen, Aberdeen University Press, 1983.

ROBERT FERGUSSON (1750–74)

235 *The Poems of Robert Fergusson*, ed. Matthew P. McDiarmid, 2 Volumes, Edinburgh, Blackwood for the Scottish Text Society, 1954–56.

This again is a major contribution to textual scholarship and McDiarmid's Introduction to his text is one of the best essays in this century on any aspect of Scottish literature.

236 *Poems by Allan Ramsay and Robert Fergusson*, eds. Alexander Manson Kinghorn and Alexander Law, Edinburgh, Scottish Academic Press for the Association for Scottish Literary Studies, 1974. Paperback edition, 1985, in the Scottish Classics series.

237 *Robert Fergusson, Scots Poems*, ed. Alexander Law, Edinburgh, Oliver & Boyd for The Saltire Society, 1947. Reprinted 1974. The Saltire Classics series.

Cassettes

238 *Robert Fergusson*, Glasgow, Scotsoun, 1974, 3 tapes, SSC 001, SSC 006, SSC 007.

Robert Fergusson's poetry has been reassessed and highly praised in this century after being so overwhelmingly overshadowed by the greatness of Robert Burns. His early death – at only twenty-four – was a tragic blow for a metropolitan Scottish poetry which could have balanced the great rural poetry of Burns. As David Daiches excellently writes in his essay in Kinsley's *Scottish Poetry*, 38 above, 'Fergusson was the only Scots poet of his century to be able to look contemporary civilisation in the eye. He knew where he stood and what he wanted to do. But he founded no school. The future lay with

Burns and the rustic tradition'. All true, and the importance of Fergusson should be widely recognised in a way that even yet it has not been. In his sparklingly stimulating Introduction to his *The Penguin Anthology of Scottish Poetry*, 67 above, Tom Scott writes, 'He is the best poet, in Scots after Montgomerie and the most promising in Scots-English after Thomson . . . he was unquestionably a major poet.' Within the Scots tradition Fergusson is certainly an important poet but it is wishful thinking to project onto him what might have been if he had lived. Many a young genius has written no major work later in a long life, but in his Introduction to 235 above Matthew P. McDiarmid hints that if Fergusson had been given more time to write poetry which matched what he had already written, he could have equalled the greatness of Dunbar. Interestingly McDiarmid does not think, if I read him aright, that Fergusson could have equalled the greatness of Burns. Nevertheless for a few years, truly only a few months, Robert Fergusson was the Villon of Edinburgh, even if at a lesser level of greatness. In terms of the Scots tradition he is a great poet.

239 *Robert Fergusson 1750-1774*, ed. Sydney Goodsir Smith, Edinburgh, Nelson, 1952.
A good collection of essays by various writers.

240 Allan H. MacLaine, *Robert Fergusson*, New York, Twayne Publishers, 1965. English Authors series.

241 Tom Scott, 'A Review of Fergusson's Poems', *Akros*. no. 6, December 1967.

242 David Daiches, *Robert Fergusson*, Edinburgh, Scottish Academic Press, 1982. Scottish Writers series.

243 F.W. Freeman, *Robert Fergusson and the Scots Humanist Compromise*, Edinburgh, Edinburgh University Press, 1984.
A brilliant book even if you should disagree with much of it. It can be supplemented or approached through Dr Freeman's essay 'Robert Fergusson: Pastoral and Politics at Mid Century', in 27(b) above.

244 Edwin Morgan, 'Robert Fergusson' in Edwin Morgan, *Crossing the Border: Essays on Scottish Literature*, Manchester. Carcanet, 1990. Bicentenary Lecture, University of Edinburgh, October 1974.

ROBERT BURNS (1759–96)

245a *The Poems and Songs of Robert Burns*, ed. James Kinsley, 3 Volumes, Oxford, Clarendon Press, 1968. Oxford English Texts.
At long last an edition which in its modern scholarship matches the greatness of the poems. The third volume is superb commentary. It reveals Professor Kinsley as a textual scholar who is also a major critic of Burns's poetry.

245b *Burns: Poems and Songs*, ed. James Kinsley, London, Oxford University Press, 1969. Oxford Standard Authors. Paperback edition 1971. Reprinted.

This one-volume edition omits the *apparatus criticus* and textual commentary of the above three-volume edition but gives the first-rate text of that edition which is based on a critical review of all the accessible manuscripts and early printings.

246 *Robert Burns*, eds. Henry W. Meikle and William Beattie, Harmondsworth, Penguin Books, 1946. Revised editions have followed.

A selection of the poems. It is adequate but, finally, not what I want in a selection of Burns's poems.

247 *A Choice of Burns's Poems and Songs*, ed. Sydney Goodsir Smith, London, Faber & Faber, 1966. Reprinted.

Again this seems to me to give a partial view of Burns which is perhaps revealed in the fact that Sydney Goodsir Smith omits 'The Vision' entirely, not that the extract in Meikle and Beattie above is of much value since the poem is not suitable for chopping into extracts.

248 *The Letters of Robert Burns*, second edition ed. G. Ross Roy, 2 Volumes, Oxford, Clarendon Press, 1985. The first edition was edited by J. De Lancey Ferguson in 1931 but this is a newly collated edition.

Cassettes and LPs

249 *Poems of Robert Burns*, Introduction and Notes by Thomas Crawford, Glasgow, Scotsoun, 1977. SSC 035-037, 3 tapes.

250 *The Songs of Robert Burns*, sung by Jean Redpath, Vermont, Philo, 1976 – continuing. Available on both LPs and cassettes. Vols. 1–7 are available in the UK on Greentrax Records of Edinburgh on both LPs and cassettes. LP nos. TRAX 017, 018, 006, 007, 008, 005, 029. The cassettes have the same numbers preceded by CTRAX. Vol. 8 will be available in the UK in 1991.

This is a major interpretation of the songs by both singer and arranger, the latter being Serge Hovey.

251 *The Miller's Reel: A Love Story from the Songs and Letters of Robert Burns*, devised by Donald Campbell, London, BBC Enterprises, 1989. REH 737.

The songs are sung by Jean Redpath and Rod Paterson in arrangements by Serge Hovey.

What can one say of the poetry of Robert Burns that has not already been said? Perhaps it is important to repeat that it is essential not to be put off by the accounts of non-literary activities which surround the poetry and the man. Although it should not need saying of a great poet, this is high art and not simply a straight re-creation of what already existed; it is the world transformed by a poetic imagination and intelligence of the highest order. The influence of Burns has been savagely attacked in this century but this should not mask recognition that Burns is the greatest of Scottish poets. Leave the years of 'shot kail' to his imitators.

The continuing reassessment of Burns's poetry increasingly shows him to have a wider range and an awareness of the art and technique of high-art poetry than even his most enthusiastic and intellectual critics had fully understood. His unique projection of man's humanity in his poetry and songs has not been undermined by these new insights into his poetry; neither has the strength of his biting satire, nor the vigour of his vernacualar Scots which his technique fully exploited. This reassessment is not an attempt to under-estimate the worth of poetry that is popular as well as great, such as 'Tam o' Shanter' or 'Holy Willie's Prayer'. Nor does it under-estimate the greatness of 'To a Louse' or 'The Jolly Beggars'. This criticism points to a poem such as 'The Vision' which has a superb range of language levels and tones; it succeeds not least because the poet employed both formal-seeming Augustan English, almost high-flown language, and varying registers of Scots to give a mixture of high and low, heich and laich, that has many levels, but in the complete art form is a single unified multiplicity that only a great poem can be in its bringing together of seeming opposites. This merging of heich and laich is evident throughout Scottish poetry from Henryson to many poets of this century, including Hugh MacDiarmid, Sydney Goodsir Smith and Robert Garioch. But also the reassessment of Burns has emphasised that those who naively think that his 'view' of Scotland is that of a 'real' world, have grossly under-estimated his achievement as a sophisticated maker of art forms. In his poetry we do not have, any more than in most great poetry, simple description or reportage; this is not realism alone. His 'Scotland', his 'Ayrshire', did not exist before he made the reality that is the poetry. And his language did not exist either; the amalgam of high Scots, low Scots, Scoto-English, formal English of the English poets, and the various other levels of colloquial and formal language did not exist till he fashioned it. And one of the limitations of the minor versifiers who imitated him was that they took only the level that is colloquial Scots. Also, of course they were not even, mostly, versifiers in any technical sense. One of the most important of recent critics who have reassessed the poetry of Burns is Carol McGuirk. She brings to her writings on Burns a recognition that he is as other great poets of the world and not only a great rustic poet within the Scottish tradition. So I can do no better than quote a quite long paragraph from her essay, in no. 27(b) above. This I believe to be not only central to an understanding of the true greatness of Robert Burns, but also important to future developments within Scottish poetry in that such critical understandings can generate a renewed will in today's Scots-writing poets to make their world as real, through the unreality of poetry, as Burns made his, and to have critics who will respond to their poetry in both its Scottish and its international reality.

In 'Notes toward a Supreme Fiction', Wallace Stevens wrote: 'From this the poem springs: That we live in a place/That is not our own and, much more, not ourselves.' This suggests a central issue about Burns and Scotland — about this poet and his 'place'. Stevens's modern assumption that poems spring from the poet's estranged effort to remake coherent meaning through deployment of different levels of language is quite applicable to Burns; though to accept that assumption is to give Burns credit for a level of coherence that posterity has preferred to deny him. But once it be acknowledged that Burns's method is not descriptive (in any simple sense) and that his methods are those of other conscious artists, the cult of personality dissipates and it becomes possible to perceive and value Burns's brilliant transfiguration (not transcription) of folk tradition. It becomes possible to grant Robert Burns what we grant other poets: the assumption that his poems spring out of a relationship not with one particular place but with the world — insofar as a world can be evoked in language. The simple truth is that Burns, no less than his countrymen Henryson or Dunbar, is a Makar, a creator. His goal is to discover (recover) meaning, not to describe simple scenes. His mode is *poesis*, not *mimesis*. Beyond the hero and the victim, in short, was the creative power that summoned and shaped those images.

252 David Daiches, *Robert Burns*, Edinburgh, Spurbooks, 1981. Reprint of revised 1966 edition. First published 1950.

253 T. Crawford, *Burns: A Study of the Poems and Songs*, Edinburgh, James Thin, The Mercat Press, 1978. A facsimile of the second edition published in 1965. Originally published in 1960 by Oliver & Boyd. An excellent critical study.

254 *Robert Burns: The Critical Heritage*, ed. Donald A. Low, London, Routledge & Kegan Paul, 1974.
From the earliest writing on Burns to Emerson's comments in January 1859.

255 *Critical Essays on Robert Burns*, ed. Donald A. Low, London, Routledge & Kegan Paul, 1975.
256 *The Art of Robert Burns*, eds. R.D.S. Jack and Andrew Noble, London and Totowa, N.J., Vision and Barnes & Noble, 1982.
257 Carol McGuirk, *Robert Burns and the Sentimental Era*, Athens, Georgia, University of Georgia Press, 1985.
    A major work.
258 Donald A. Low, *Robert Burns*, Edinburgh, Scottish Academic Press, 1986. Scottish Writers series.

B. EIGHTEENTH-CENTURY ANGLO-SCOTS POETS

James Thomson, listed below, is incomparably the best of the Anglo-Scots of this period. Indeed I find it difficult to recommend the poetry of any of the others writing at this time in a Scoto-English.

There is Robert Blair (1699–1746) whose poem *The Grave* appeals to my interest in the morbid, but it fails to win me over. The poem will, however, be remembered because of William Blake's illustrations for the 1808 edition; the first edition is dated 1743. The extracts from this moral tale in *The Oxford Book of Eighteenth Century Verse* are well chosen.

The Jacobite William Hamilton of Bangour (1704–1754) wrote insipid verse. His imitation ballad 'The Braes of Yarrow' appears in *Longer Scottish Poems, Volume II*, 81 above, and the anthologists describe it as 'memorable poetry'.

James Beattie (1735–1803) is of interest for cultural and sociological reasons. He was Professor of Moral Philosophy and Logic at Aberdeen University. He reveals the language and cultural insecurities of many poets of his time. He rejected Scots as a language suitable for his own serious poetry and so wrote his poem of high aim, *The Minstrel*, 1771, 1774, in English; it is now mostly unread. He issued a book of Scotticisms, 1779, to assist his fellow Scots to cleanse their writings of these barbarous words. But Beattie was most helpful to Alexander Ross in assisting him to get his *Helenore* published. He even wrote a poem to be printed in Ross's Scots masterpiece, and it is in Scots, and a Scots with a North-east flavour at that. And irony of ironies, this is the poem by which Beattie is now remembered. It is in many anthologies, entitled 'To Mr Alexander Ross of Lochlea' (see 66 and 67 above). No doubt Beattie would have preferred to be remembered by his *The Minstrel*, extracts from which are in *Longer Scottish Poems, Volume II*, 81 above. The editors write, however, that they include these extracts 'for historical reasons: *The Minstrel* is almost as important as "Ossian" for both English and European romanticism'.

It could be said that Beattie and Blair and other poets who attempted to write in English sacrificed their chances of writing major poetry by turning their backs on their mother tongue – Scots. They were split down the middle in cultural schisms and insecurities. They could also be seen to have undermined the Scots tradition, and by so doing made it more difficult for later poets to attempt important poetry in Scots. But of course later poets have been able to overcome that diminishment of their cultural base. And also, if Beattie and Blair failed in a Scoto-English then James Thomson succeeded; but he might have been an even greater poet in his native Scots.

JAMES THOMSON (1700–48)

259 *James Thomson: The Seasons*, ed. James Sambrook, Oxford, Clarendon Press, 1981.
Now the standard edition.

260 *James Thomson: Liberty, The Castle of Indolence and Other Poems*, ed. James Sambrook, Oxford, Clarendon Press, 1986. Oxford English Texts.
Now the standard edition.

An earlier editor of James Thomson's poems was J. Logie Robertson and his *James Thomson: The Seasons and the Castle of Indolence*, Oxford, 1891, remains of quite considerable value for its editor's notes and commentary on Thomson's use of Scots vocabulary and usages. Robertson also indicates Scottish literary associations and themes. He also edited *The Complete Poetical Works of James Thomson*, Oxford, 1908, Oxford Standard Author series.

In his poem, 'Extempore – on some Commemorations of Thomson', Robert Burns wrote in the first verse,

> Dost thou not rise, indignant Shade,
>   And smile wi' spurning scorn,
> When they wha wad hae starv'd thy life,
>   Thy senseless turf adorn. –

So, as with his better-known lines in 'To William Simpson, Ochiltree' on the failure of Scottish society to support Robert Fergusson, Burns saw James Thomson as having suffered similar rejection by the powers-that-be in the land that gave him the education and upbringing that were the sources of his poetry. Unlike James VI and his band of poets following at his heels to London, who went for reasons of high ambition, there is little doubt that Thomson went to London for two reasons: a lack of patronage in Scotland and the claustrophobia of its literary scene. The situation has changed little to this day. Of course, when Thomson arrived in London, like many another he trimmed his Scottish sails, not least with regard to his language. But Burns had no doubt of the essential Scottishness of Thomson's poetry; nor do I.

The Scottish aspects of his poetry, apart from the obvious links to the Nature Prologues of Gavin Douglas, were until recently not given sufficient critical analysis, certainly not by non-Scottish critics, but now that has been corrected by the work by Mary Jane W. Scott which I list below. Critics who have been part of the movement for the re-establishment of an independent Scottish literary tradition have tended to emphasise the Scottishness of the great poets, not least with regard to their language – the auld makars were praised for their Scots being a truly national language. Burns, on the other hand, was attacked for corrupting his Scots with English and to this day poets are attacked for this; for being, supposedly, unfaithful to the independent Scots tradition. In fact, the auld makars used a mixture of powerful native Scots, aureate Latin diction and Southern English. That is the linguistic reality and it is an extension of language that is also in Burns, if in a different way. It is also an absolute characteristic of Hugh MacDiarmid's poetry, whether in English or in Scots. Not a few modern poets have recognised with MacDiarmid that Scots takes in English. So also Thomson's poetry reveals this push towards an enrichment of language. His heavy use of Latinisms, well beyond the practice of his English contemporaries, is an aspect of both his Scottish educational background and the Scottish literary tradition. This, allied to his being in the line of Scottish nature poets who stood apart from such a poetry in the English tradition, reveals his essential Scottishness, as does much else in the poetry. All this is most admirably revealed in Dr Scott's book.

In her essay in Kinsley's *Scottish Poetry*, 38 above, on 'The Scottish Augustans', A.M. Oliver writes, 'Thomson has always been the poet of *The Seasons*. This is unfortunate, for, despite the abiding worth of that monumental miscellany, *The Castle of Indolence* is finer and more sustained poetry.' But Dr Scott is perhaps fairer in her essay in 27(b) above when she writes that *The Castle of Indolence* 'ranks with *The Seasons* as an Anglo-Scottish masterpiece'. Finally, however, I go back to the first shorter version of 'Winter' as the peak of Thomson's achievement. For the full text of this see *Longer Scottish Poems,*

Volume II, 81 above. The influence of Thomson is powerfully seen throughout later English poetry and so, both in his own poetry and in his influence on others, Thomson has changed the way we see the world. As Douglas Grant says in a most excellent ending to his book on Thomson listed below, 'We are for ever meeting the shadow of his presence as we read, or look out upon Nature'.

261 Douglas Grant, *James Thomson: Poet of 'The Seasons'*, London, Cresset Press, 1951.

262 Mary Jane W. Scott, *James Thomson: Anglo-Scot*, Athens, Georgia, The University of Georgia Press, 1988.

C. EIGHTEENTH-CENTURY GAELIC POETS

In his *Progress and Poetry*, 18 above, John MacQueen indicates the confidence in the old Gaelic order by seventeenth-century poets such as Mary MacLeod and Iain Lom. He sees Culloden and the reprisals that followed finally putting an end to such confidence and also to, he writes, 'the poetic style in which it had found expression.' But Professor MacQueen continues, 'It is remarkable how swift a rebirth followed'.

ALASDAIR MAC MHAIGHSTIR ALASDAIR
(ALEXANDER MACDONALD) (*c.*1700–1770)

263 *The Poems of Alexander MacDonald*, eds. A. and A. MacDonald, Inverness, Northern Counties Newspaper and Publishing Co. Ltd, 1924.

The first evidence of the eighteenth-century rebirth of Gaelic poetry after Culloden, which in a very real way sprang out of the hatred engendered by the attempt to suppress Gaelic culture by Lowland Scottish and English Hanoverians alike, was the publication of a book of poems by Alasdair Mac Mhaighstir Alasdair in 1751. It was entitled, with a deliberation that was both political and cultural – if these two entities can ever be separated – *Ais-eiridh na Sean Chánoin Albannaich* ('Resurrection of the Ancient Scottish Tongue'). So yet again we come to a Scottish poet, in his own terms, proclaiming a renaissance. And this was one which, without losing touch with the old orders of Gaelic poetry, did also make it new.

Mac Mhaighstir Alasdair was a man of fierce passions. Although a teacher employed by the Society in Scotland for Propagating Christian Knowledge who became an elder of the Reformed Kirk, he did not let such matters inhibit his poetry. The employers of this great poet were to note in 1744 that the schoolmaster of

Ardnamurchan was 'an offence to all Sober Well-inclined persons as he wanders thro' the Country composing Galick songs, stuffed with obscene language'.

Politically Mac Mhaighstir Alasdair was an extreme Jacobite and John Lorne Campbell writes in his anthology, *Highland Songs of the Forty-Five*, 1933 (2nd edition, Edinburgh, Scottish Academic Press for the Scottish Gaelic Texts Society, 1984), 'the invective he heaped on the reigning House and its supporters gained him the enthusiastic approval of friends and the severe displeasure of the Government'. According to the editors of the 1924 book, 263 above, although numerous copies of his 1751 book 'were burnt at the Cross of Edinburgh by the common hangman, the author himself escaped unscathed'. But the poet was as much a propagandist for Gaelic culture as for the Jacobite cause.

Sadly the reverend editors of his great and varied poetry did not let it go unscathed. His satires are scurrilously magnificent, sparing no local worthy or rival bard, nor the delicate tastes of any reader in their most vivid and explicit imagery. Some of his love poems were likely to offend much earthier men than the editors of the 1924 edition of his poetry who wrote, 'these filthy rhymes will remain a blot for ever on the memory of the bard' – and so they suppressed them. But in other ways they got it right, 'There is no other that can be compared to him in the whole range of Gaelic literature, as indeed there is none like him'. Five years later Aodh de Blácam in his *Gaelic Literature Surveyed* writes, 'He is the most individual, the boldest of Scottish singers'. And in 1987 Professor Derick Thomson, in his essay in 27(b) above, writes of this great poet, 'He had the intellectual strength to forge a style and a purpose of his own from indigenous and imported elements, yet combine this with emotional power and also with an earthiness and coarseness that are equally remarkable'.

His editors in their edition of 1924 preferred his nature poetry, including 'Oran an t-Samhraidh' ('Song to Summer') which they saw as 'one of the greatest efforts of the Gaelic muse'. This is indeed vibrant poetry. And so also is his great and justly famous 'Moladh Móraig' ('Praise of Morag'). This is a unique poem, at least for a Lowlander such as me. It is richly powerful with what Sorley MacLean has termed 'its paeans of lust', and Dr MacLean suggests further of this great poem, 'I suppose no Celtic Twilightist ever read "Moladh Móraig". Its abandoned *joie-de-vivre*, its physical glow, its amazing virtuosity of technique makes it par excellence a Gaelic poem of the great period. Imagine Mórag swathed in a tenuous halo of the Twilight: Mórag is a creature of the real world that is full of self-confidence, a real world that jeers at papal asceticism in its exultation in the physical splendour of a woman. No wonder it carried the douce circumspect John Mackenzie off his feet. That is the nature of Alexander MacDonald's realism; he exaggerates qualities that are purely tangible. The result is a kind of physical apotheosis that differs from reality, not in nature but in degree.' This noble tribute is from Sorley MacLean's pioneering paper 'Realism in Gaelic Poetry'[1],reprinted in his *Ris a' Bhruthaich*, 56 above.

The most famous poem by Mac Mhaighstir Alasdair, and the one often regarded as his most important single poem, is 'Birlinn Chlann Raghnaill' ('Clanranald's Galley'). This is one of the great poems in any language, crafted as if by an old bard but also taking Gaelic poetry into new areas of personal understanding, and by so doing raising a great tradition to even greater heights. Of 'Birlinn Chlann Raghnaill' Derick Thomson has written in his *An Introduction to Gaelic Poetry*, 39 above, 'There is no slackness or flabbiness of thought or expression here. The verse is hard, terse and businesslike, the clean rhythm of the lines like the movement of sea-water along the side of a boat. This poem is the ultimate demonstration of Mac Mhaighstir Alasdair's hard, exact intellectual power.'

In addition to the writings of Professor Thomson and Dr Sorley MacLean to which I have referred above, there is also Ronald Black's *Mac Mhaighstir Alasdair: The Ardnamurchan Years* which is an attractive introduction; it takes the story up to 1745 (The Society of West Highland and Island Historical Research, 1986). There is a chapter, 'Alexander MacDonald and Duncan Macintyre', in Malcolm Chapman's *The Gaelic Vision in Scottish Culture*, 1978. A small book on MacDonald by Sheila Duffy was published in 1982, but it says little about the poetry.

264 J.L. Campbell, 'The Expurgating of Mac Mhaighstir Alasdair', *Scottish Gaelic Studies*, vol. 12, part 1, 1971.

ROB DONN (ROBERT MACKAY) (1715–78)

265 *Songs and Poems in the Gaelic Language*, ed. Hew Morrison, Edinburgh, John Grant, 1899.

At the end of his fine book on Rob Donn listed below, Ian Grimble writes, 'the corpus of poetry that he did bequeath to posterity entitles him to the highest place amongst the illiterate peasant poets of Europe'. And Donald Sage wrote, to quote from Ian Grimble, 'He

---

[1]This paper, although printed in *Transactions of the Gaelic Society of Inverness*, vol. 37, 1934-6, Inverness, Northern Counties Newspaper and Publishing Co. Ltd, 1946, was delivered on 19th April 1938.

stood alone. His poetry is history — a history of everyone and everything with which he at any time came in contact in the country in which he lived. His descriptions do not merely let us know what these things or persons were, but as things that are.'

Rob Donn is an observer of people, ironic in his intelligent appreciation of inter-personal and social relationships. Iain Crichton Smith, in his brief but stimulating essay, 'A Note on Gaelic Criticism' in 58 above, sees him as 'perhaps the most essentially modern of Gaelic writers in the centuries previous to our own . . . If poetry in the end is a statement about being human, in language that is moving and interesting, then Rob Donn is one of our most important poets, in many ways our most important'.

In the late thirties, in his essay 'Realism in Gaelic Poetry', 56 above, Sorley MacLean revealed that he had no high regard for Rob Donn's poetry and in the early eighties (see the essay 'Some Thoughts about Gaelic Poetry', again 56 above) he asked, 'how can such relaxed poetry be great? . . . Lack of intensity and passion, indeed lack of the *lacrimae rerum*, is manifest in Rob Donn's poetry'.

In my less-informed response to this poetry, I believe that the apparent lack of tension in it is what strengthens my awareness of its underlying power. There, of course, I reveal my own inclinations as a poet. But for a concluding statement on the poetry of Rob Donn I would turn again to Derick Thomson who, in writing on its social aspects, says, 'there is no earlier body of Gaelic verse from which we can get so many-sided a picture of people in a community, with the tensions and sanctions that affect their lives'. Professor Thomson goes on to point to some trivial detail in this portrayal, and also to some trivial verse, but concludes, 'There can be little doubt that it represents an important peak of achievement in Gaelic poetry'.

266 Donald J. MacLeod, 'The Poetry of Rob Donn Mackay', *Scottish Gaelic Studies*, vol. 12, part 1, 1971.

267 Ian Grimble, *The World of Rob Donn*, Edinburgh, The Edina Press, 1979.

DONNCHADH BAN MAC AN T-SAOIR (DUNCAN BAN MACINTYRE) (1724–1812)

268 *Orain Dhonnchaidh Bhàin. The Songs of Duncan Ban Macintyre*, ed. Aonghas MacLeòid, Edinburgh, Oliver & Boyd for the Scottish Gaelic Texts Society, 1952. Reprinted by the Scottish Academic Press for the Society, 1978.

A very good translation of 'Moladh Beinn Dòbhrain' ('The Praise of Ben Dorain') into English has been made by Iain Crichton Smith. It was published, *Ben Dorain*, Preston, Akros Publications, 1969.

Reprinted, Newcastle upon Tyne, Northern House, 1988. Donnchadh Bàn, in contrast to the formally educated and, in conventional terms, cultured Mac Mhaighstir Alasdair, could neither read nor write. But, of course, in terms of poetry an oral tradition can nurture great poets as admirably as a culture of the written or printed word. And the poetry of this 'illiterate', in modern terms, is a major achievement in any culture. As well as being of the oral tradition, Donnchadh Bàn spent much of his life outside his own Gaelic society, as a soldier in the Lowlands and a member of the Edinburgh City Guard. Nevertheless he is best known for his nature poetry, which is rich in detail and in superb observation. To many people he is, indeed, the poet of 'Beinn Dòbhrain', rightly seen as one of the finest and greatest of Gaelic poems.

But this is not a one-poem poet, although at the highest level of, say, his great forerunner Mac Mhaighstir Alasdair, a poet of only a small number of fully-achieved poems. He is at his greatest in two poems: 'Oran Coire a' Cheathaich' ('The Song of the Misty Corrie') and 'Moladh Beinn Dòbhrain' ('The Praise of Ben Dorain'). The key subject-matter of both poems is the deer. Before moving to the Lowlands the poet was employed as a forester or gamekeeper by Campbell aristocrats and he knew the deer forest of the mountains of Perthshire-Argyllshire in the closest detail.

Unlike Mac Mhaighstir Alasdair, and a good many modern Gaelic poets, Donnchadh Bàn was not a man to challenge the established order; he knew his place. That is a cruel phrase and quite unimportant to the two great poems, except that his very acceptance of the 'natural order' of social structure as well as of nature was a strength to the poet. He looks at, and takes, the world as it is — or at least the world of Nature. This includes accepting the dogs of the hunt savaging his beloved deer. In his Introduction to his translation of 'Beinn Dòbhrain' Iain Crichton Smith writes, 'and the marvellous thing is that there is no moral'. This indeed is a stance that is part of this poem's greatness, but I am sure that Iain Crichton Smith is not suggesting that this is the poetry of an innocent. Great poets, at some level where intuition and reasoning intellect merge, know what they are doing in their poems. And this is the work of a major poet. The honesty of this poetry and of the poet facing the reality of the world means, Iain Crichton Smith suggests, that 'We have to return to the classics to find anything comparable to this landscape of sun and reality and truth'. Sorley MacLean saw 'Beinn Dòbhrain' as 'Exquisitely brilliant and subtle in technique, it is in content, I believe, the greatest example of naturalistic realism in the poetry of Europe. Naturalism is not generally the realism of poetry, but here it undoubtedly is.'

269 Iain Crichton Smith, 'Duncan Ban Macintyre', *The Scotsman*, 20th March, 1974. Reprinted in *Towards the Human*, Loanhead, Macdonald, 1986.

270 Iain Crichton Smith, 'Donnchadh Bàn Mac an t-Saoir', *Gairm*, no. 118, Spring 1982.

UILLEAM ROS (WILLIAM ROSS) (1762–90)

271 *Orain Ghàidhealach. Gaelic Songs*, collected by John Mackenzie, new edition, ed. George Calder, Edinburgh, Oliver & Boyd, 1937. First published, edited by John Mackenzie, Inverness, printed by R. Carruthers, for Lewis Grant and D. MacCulloch, 1830.

Ros's editor believed him to be influenced by the love poems of Robert Burns, and exceeding the Lowland poet in frankness. This is rather too close to the lowering response to Burns as a romantic figure in a local tradition of poetry for a proper assessment of the poetry of Ros. There was quite a legend of his loves which was current even in his own short lifetime. He was said to have died for love. More probably it was TB. But, factually, he did meet a woman whom he was passionate about and who went off to marry a sea captain and live in Liverpool. But although the love poems of Ros are his major achievements, Derick Thomson also refers to a 'strong representation of humorous, witty and bawdy verse in his work'.

So also there is a strain of 'romantic' poems but beyond that there is a group of love poems that could only be regarded as 'romantic' by the most sentimental of readers. Derick Thomson has written of a poem that seems to have been largely ignored by other critics; I refer to 'Oran eadar am Bàrd agus Cailleach-mhilleadh-nan-dàn' ('Song between the Poet and the Hag-who-spoils Songs'). In this poem the poet of love reveals his understanding of the twisting coils of life and love within that life. In this debate between the poet and the Hag the latter, as Derick Thomson says, 'wins hands down'. And the poet reveals he understands very well, through his satire and realistic view of himself, the dangers of being the subject of a mythology that portrays him as a legendary love poet. This self-awareness was an essential part of his great and tragic love poems.

There are only a very few of these great love poems by Ros. Of these I would refer to 'Feasgar Luain' ('Monday Evening'), but the greatest of Ros's poems is 'Oran Eile' ('Another Song'). For me to write of this poem in the shadow of its greatest admirer would be impertinence. I refer to Sorley MacLean who has written of a characteristic of Ros's poetry being 'a lofty passionate ardour, which in his greatest poem, 'Oran Eile air a' Mhodh Cheudna', becomes a cry of anguish expressed in language almost as stately as a Greek sculpture or a MacCrimmon pìobaireachd. This last song of Ross is to me almost unaccountable in its blend of emotion and art. It is in essence one of the saddest poems ever conceived; it expresses not the sadness of disillusion with life; it is a more poignant sadness, the farewell to life and joy of a young man who is terribly in love with life. It is realist in its poignancy, in its complete lack of irrelevancies, but nevertheless it is a highly sophisticated poem in its musical elaboration and its chiselled perfection of line. The strange thing about it to me is that such a perfection of self-conscious technique should accompany such poignancy of emotion. Of such a poem it seems pointless to say that it is realist although it is clearly unromantic. To me it has the completeness of the largest utterance of Shakespeare . . .'[1]

IAIN MACCODRUM (*c*.1693–1779)

272 *The Songs of John MacCodrum: Bard to Sir James MacDonald of Sleat*, ed. William Matheson, Edinburgh, Oliver & Boyd for the Scottish Gaelic Texts Society, 1938. A new edition is in preparation.

One of the last, if not the last, of the professional poets – he became Bard to Sir James MacDonald of Sleat when he was about seventy years old – and celebrated for his 'incisive wit and keen eye', MacCodrum is North Uist's most notable bard. His great song 'Smeòrach Chlann Dòmhnaill' ('The Mavis of Clan Donald') is still widely sung today.

273 Donald Archie MacDonald, 'Ath-sgrùdadh: Iain MacCodrum' ('Re-assessment: John MacCodrum'), *Gairm*, nos. 129 and 130, Winter 1984 and Spring 1985.

[1] From Sorley MacLean's essay, 'Realism in Gaelic Poetry', first published in *Transactions of the Gaelic Society of Inverness*, vol. 37, 1934–6, Inverness, Northern Counties Newspaper and Publishing Co. Ltd, 1946. Although printed in a volume of *Transactions*, 1934–6, Sorley MacLean's paper to the Society was delivered on 19th April, 1938.

SECTION VII
Nineteenth-Century Poets

JAMES HOGG (1770–1835)

274 *Selected Poems*, ed. J.W. Oliver, Edinburgh, Oliver & Boyd, for The Saltire Society, 1940. The Saltire Classics.

275 *Selected Poems*, ed. Douglas S. Mack, Oxford, Clarendon Press, 1970. An important pioneering selection.

276 *Selected Poems and Songs*, ed. David Groves, Edinburgh, Scottish Academic Press, 1986.

A first-rate work of selection and scholarship.

There are *The Poetical Works of the Ettrick Shepherd*, 5 Volumes, Glasgow, Edinburgh, and London, Blackie & Son, 1838-40, and *The Works of the Ettrick Shepherd*, ed. Thomas Thomson, 2 Volumes, London, Edinburgh and Glasgow, Blackie & Son, 1865. Volume 2 is Poems and Life.

I believe that a 'Selected Poems and Songs' volume is the best approach to Hogg's poetry. The first modern selection of worth is Douglas S. Mack's, 275 above, and David Groves's selection is an excellent book by which to approach the work, not least for reproducing the music of the songs, including some composed by Hogg himself. Hogg as a poet is first-rate when at his best, but truly awful when he is bad.

Longer Scottish Poems, Volume II, 81 above, has a first-rate selection of Hogg's longer poems with the madly extravagant excellence of 'The Witch of Fife', the unique 'Kilmeny' and the less well-known 'May of the Moril Glen' which the anthologists describe most accurately as 'rollicking and exuberant satire, directed at male sexuality, that deflates by inflation'. The long middle section of 'Kilmeny' has often been dismissed as pedestrian and out of place in a poem that begins as visionary. The beginning and end of the poem can, indeed, be seen as amongst the finest passages in Scottish poetry but I agree with the anthologists that the historical allegory section in the middle of the poem is 'profoundly Scottish, in the tradition of Ramsay's "The Vision"'. The whole poem is a unique achievement and deserves to be read in full, not carved up as in so many anthologies. It is, to quote Douglas Mack, 'the achievement of a poet of considerable importance'.

The best of Hogg's songs are also first-rate; there is the famous 'When the Kye comes Hame' and 'A Boy's Song', to confine myself to what current consensus opinion designates as the very best.

277 Louis Simpson, *James Hogg: A Critical Study*, Edinburgh, Oliver & Boyd, 1962.

278 Douglas Gifford, *James Hogg*, Edinburgh, Ramsay Head Press, 1976. A good introduction to the prose as well as the poetry; perhaps Hogg is at his greatest in *The Private Memoirs and Confessions of a Justified Sinner*, not that I would wish to underestimate either the poetry or the vast range of other prose works of this still under-valued genius. Douglas Mack writes in *ScotLit*, no. 1, March 1989, the Newsletter of the Association for Scottish Literary Studies, of plans for a new collected edition of Hogg.

279 David Groves, *James Hogg: The Growth of a Writer*, Edinburgh, Scottish Academic Press, 1988.

SIR WALTER SCOTT (1771–1832)

280 *The Poetical Works of Sir Walter Scott, Bart.*, ed. J.G. L[ockhart], 12 Volumes, Edinburgh, Robert Cadell, 1833–34.

281 *The Poetical Works*, ed. J. Logie Robertson, Oxford, Oxford University Press, reprinted 1967. Oxford Standard Authors. An almost unreadable edition that goes back to 1904 in its tight typography.

282 *Selected Poems*, ed. Thomas Crawford, Oxford, Clarendon Press, 1972.

In Canto 4 of *Childe Harold's Pilgrimage* Byron referred to Scott as the Ariosto of the North and to Ariosto as the southern Scott who also 'Sang, ladye-love and war, romance and knightly worth'. *Orlando Furioso* remains living poetry but Scott's romances are revealed, I believe, as being not even narratives that we can accept as authentic now. For long I had the belief that Scott was, admittedly by the highest standards, a poet of only one poem – 'Proud Maisie'. *Longer Scottish Poems, Volume II*, 81 above, has a very good selection of Scott's poetry, and I almost think from reading its long extract from *Marmion* that Scott was a better poet, at least in that book, than I had judged. In his Introduction to the *Selected Poems*, 282 above, Thomas Crawford, one of the editors of *Longer Scottish Poems*, suggests, 'it is no longer possible to claim *Marmion* as Scott's poetical masterpiece'. In his selection, 282 above, Mr Crawford prints *The Lay of the Last Minstrel* and *The Lady of the Lake* in full.

283 Nancy M. Goslee, 'Marmion and the Metaphor of Forgery', Scottish Literary Journal, vol. 7, no. 1, May 1980.

284 J.H. Alexander, 'Marmion': Studies in Interpretation and Composition, Salzburg, Salzburg Studies in English Literature, 1981.

285 Paul Henderson Scott, Walter Scott and Scotland, Edinburgh, Blackwood, 1981.

286 Thomas Crawford, Scott, Edinburgh, Scottish Academic Press, 1982. Scottish Writers series. A new edition, revised and elaborated, of his 1965 book.

287 Nancy Moore Goslee, Scott the Rhymer, Lemington, The University Press of Kentucky, 1988.

WILLIAM TENNANT (1784–1848)

288 The Comic Poems of William Tennant, eds. Alexander Scott and Maurice Lindsay, Edinburgh, Scottish Academic Press for the Association of Scottish Literary Studies, 1989.
Tennant was born in Anstruther in Fife and although a prolific poet most of his work is best forgotten, which is true of all minor poets. Although there may be other poems that should be restored to general circulation, the comic poems in the above book seem to be the best of Tennant; they are 'Anster Fair' and 'Papistry Storm'd' and two short farcical poems. The English of 'Anster Fair' surprises me each time I return to this poem, not in itself but because I have the idea implanted, although I know it to be not so, that this is a poem in Scots. Of course some of its rhymes show that perhaps I am not so far wrong and to have had it with Scots orthography might have given us a truer sound pattern. Much has been made of the stanza form, ottava rima, as Tennant's experimentation with it proceeded or coincided with Byron's use of the form. But that is not important with regard to the poem; the first of its six cantos is printed in Longer Scottish Poems, Volume II, 81 above. The mock epic 'Papistry Storm'd' is in Scots and is excellently returned to general availability by the Scott/Lindsay volume.

GEORGE GORDON, LORD BYRON (1788–1824)

289 The Complete Poetical Works, ed. Jerome J. McGann, 5 Volumes, Oxford, Clarendon Press, 1980-86. Also in paperback.
Now the standard edition.

290 Poems, ed. A.S.B. Glover, Harmondsworth, Penguin Books, 1954. Reprinted 1985.
A selection.

291 Don Juan, eds. T.G. Steffan, E. Steffan and W.W. Pratt, Harmondsworth, Penguin Books, 1973. Revised edition 1982.

If I underestimate the poetry of Walter Scott I probably forgive Byron all his poetic sins. I glory in the great length of *Don Juan*; perhaps only Ovid's poetry sparkles more in quite this way – vital, witty, zestful, utterly without pomposity and daringly alive beyond anything we have a right to ask of a mere mortal. Many heroes are found to have clay feet, but Byron rises above all his admirers with a quality that, although he might disapprove, I can only term saintly. In this he is with Burns, and as Scottish, which is why some English readers have had trouble in coming to terms with his poetry. For T.S. Eliot on the Scottishness of Byron see his 'Byron' in *On Poetry and Poets*, 1957.

292 Nannie Katharin Wells, *George Gordon, Lord Byron: A Scottish Genius*, Abingdon-on-Thames, The Abbey Press, 1960.
Later editions have a Foreword by Hugh MacDiarmid.

293 Roderick S. Speer, 'Byron and the Scottish Literary Tradition', *Studies in Scottish Literature*, vol. 14, 1979.

294 *Byron: Wrath and Rhyme*, ed. Alan Bold, London and Totawa, N.J., Vision and Barnes & Noble, 1983.
Includes essays by Tom Scott, 'Byron as a Scottish Poet', and Edwin Morgan, 'Voice, Tone and Transition in *Don Juan*' the later being reprinted in Morgan's *Crossing the Border*, Manchester, Carcanet, 1990.

295 Angus Calder, 'Byron and Scotland', *Cencrastus*, no. 15, New Year, 1984.

296 *Byron and Scotland: Radical or Dandy?*, ed. Angus Calder, Edinburgh, Edinburgh University Press, 1989.

UILLEAM MACDHUNLEIBHE (WILLIAM LIVINGSTONE) (1808–70)

297 *Duain agus Orain*, ed. R. Blair, Glasgow, Archibald Sinclair, 1882.
In the thirties, in his *At the Sign of the Thistle*, 43 above, Hugh MacDiarmid writes of Livingstone, 'The irresistible verve of his utterance, the savagery of his satire, are abhorrent to the spineless triflers who want pretty-prettifyings, and not any devotion to matters of life and death'. Livingstone wrote long poems aiming for epic success and whilst he often fails, they are worthy failures. John MacInnes, who is more knowledgeable than I am, is harsher than I would be on these 'epics' in his essay in 27(c) above.

Hugh MacDiarmid translated two of Livingstone's poems and his versions are printed in his *The Golden Treasury of Scottish Poetry*, 1940. They are the two poems which are recognised as Livingstone's greatest works. They are 'Eirinn a' Gul' ('Ireland Weeping') and 'Fios thun a' Bhàird' ('A Message to the Poet'). The latter is the greater poem with its modern-sounding title and an even more modern change of tone halfway through, from beautiful nature poetry to an account of the desolation of the island of Islay. In his essay, 'The Poetry of William Livingstone', 56 above, Sorley MacLean writes of this poem, 'its grandeur and perfection of grave music has a kind of finality that perhaps no other poem on the Clearances has. It may have no real originality of thought, image or even music, but its vital effect of majestic sadness and restrained anger, grandeur and simplicity makes it, as it were, the last word on the theme.' A most powerful tribute. John MacInnes sees it equally convincingly as a 'beautiful and moving poem in its marriage of craftsmanship and artistic sincerity'. R. Blair, the editor of 297 above, believes this poem 'cannot be surpassed for the sad pathos with which he laments "the things that once were" in his native island'.

298 Christopher Whyte, 'Cruth is pearsantachd am bàrdachd Uilleam MhicDhunlèibhe' ('Form and personality in the poetry of William Livingstone'), *Gairm*, no. 139, Summer 1987.

JAMES THOMSON ('B.V.') (1834–82)

299 *The Poetical Works of James Thomson (B.V.)* ed. Bertram Dobell, 2 Volumes, London, Reeves & Turner and Bertram Dobell, 1895.

There is a long introductory memoir by Dobell but it should be read in the light of William Schaefer's book, 303 below.

300 *Poems and Some Letters of James Thomson*, ed. Anne Ridler, London, Centaur Press, 1963. Centaur Classics.

This extended selection is a better volume through which to approach Thomson's poetry than the Dobell edition above which contains much unimportant poetry.

Thomson's biographers have given us a life that is tragic in its tale of depression and alcoholism. To his friends, however, he seems to have been a different man from the poet described as the 'laureate of pessimism'. He is a poet of great joy too, and we should not equate the whole life with this philosophical stance of pessimism or gloom that is revealed in the poetry. His major work remains, as popularly recognised, *The City of Dreadful Night*. The rhythms and language of this poem, first printed in parts in Charles Bradlaugh's weekly paper of 'freethinking' *The National Reformer* in 1874, remain of their time but to suggest, as some critics have, that this is mere journalism in verse is to ignore the essential quality of this important poem. It is a poem of depression and despair and of man's loneliness, not only in a modern city but in his essential separateness. The city is a most powerful and extending image for this primary human condition. For long *The City of Dreadful Night* was seem as a nihilist poem but attitudes change and today it can, perhaps, be seem as being powerfully emotional not only in its pessimism but in its revelation of human courage in facing the night that is always out there. This is a work of art, not a work of biography for all Thomson's alcoholism and tragic death, and it is the greater poem for being recognised as such.

301 Henry S. Salt, *The Life of James Thomson ('B.V.')*, revised edition, London, Watts & Co., 1914. First published in 1889.
Romanticises the life to suit the popular perception of the poetry.

302 Imogene Walker, *James Thomson (B.V.): A Critical Study*, Ithaca, Cornell University Press, 1950.

303 William David Schaefer, *James Thomson (B.V.): Beyond 'The City'*, Berkeley and Los Angeles, University of California Press, 1965. Perspectives in Criticism 17.

IAIN MAC A' GHOBHAINN (JOHN SMITH) (1848–81)

304 For the poems of Mac a' Ghobhainn see the anthology *Bàrdachd Leòdhais*, edited by Iain N. MacLeòid, Glasgow, Alasdair Mac Labhruinn, 1916. Reprinted 1955.
This is, as with so many Gaelic poets since at least the seventeenth century, a fearless political poet. Mac a' Ghobhainn speaks out against the exploitation of the Highlands for sport by rich, and often absent, landlords and visiting sportsmen. A brave man, Mac a' Ghobhainn is the author of at least two or three poems that can be considered great, particularly in the context of nineteenth-century Scottish poetry. When I first read this poetry I wondered why it had not had the recognition it demands, although, of course, known to knowledgeable Gaelic critics.

In his essay in 27(c) above John MacInnes refers to two poems by Mac a' Ghobhainn as major works. They are 'Spiorad an Uamhair' ('The Spirit of Pride') and 'Spiorad a' Charthannais' ('The Spirit of Kindliness'). In his *An Introduction to Gaelic Poetry*, 39 above, Derick Thomson writes, 'In the whole of nineteenth-century Gaelic verse this is probably the most considered and the most damning and scathing indictment we have of those policies which decimated the Gaelic people. The fearless quality of Mac a' Ghobhainn's mind shows through repeatedly.' This is so because out of his anger he created, in a controlled yet passionate language, true poetry. We urgently need a collection of his poems, and with good translations into English. By one of these matters of chance which can be so creative, after I had first read this poetry a translation into English by Iain Crichton Smith of Mac a' Ghobhainn's 'Spiorad a' Charthannais' was printed in *Cencrastus*, no. 29, Spring 1988. This could be the base of any edition with English translations. As Professor Thomson wrote of this poem, 'His greatest poem has the heartbeats of his countrymen in it, but also the pulses of their intellect, and an observer a century later may confess to a sense of relief that heart and mind combined to produce a great poem before the century was out.'

MAIRI NIC A' PHEARSAIN (MARY MACPHERSON) (1821–98)

305 *Dàin agus Orain Ghàidhlig*, Inbhir Nis, A. agus U. MacCoinnich, 1891.

306 *Màiri Mhór nan Oran: Taghadh d'a h-òrain le eachdraidh a beatha is notaichean*, ed. Dòmhnall Eachann Meek, Glaschu, Gairm, 1977.

Known as Màiri Mhór nan Oran (Big Mary of the Songs), this was a personage larger than life. She was especially taken to many people's hearts as the bard of Highland land reform, but finally, Derick Thomson suggests, see 39 above, she may be remembered as a poet for her 'evocations of Skye and the community she knew there in her youth. She belonged to the people there, and had a voice that could reach them, and that is the voice that survives.' The high regard in which she was held is reflected by the words on her gravestone, where she is described as 'The Skye Poetess' and, the inscription continues, 'Loving the Highlands and its people, ever forward in their cause by speech and song, she merited and received the affectionate regard of Highlanders'. Sorley MacLean reveals an essential quality in Màiri Mhór's poems in an essay on her work (see 56 above) when he writes of 'a strange complexity in the "simplicities" of Màiri Mhór's poetry. Perhaps it is wrong to use the word "subtle", but there are complexities that are deep if not broad. It is question-begging to use the word "simple" of what is greatly moving, and Màiri Mhór's poetry has always been greatly moving to some of the most "sophisticated" as well as to a great many of the "unsophisticated" among those who know her language.'

307 Iain Crichton Smith, 'Bàrdachd Màiri Mhór nan Oran' ('The Poetry of Mary MacPherson'), *Gairm*, 132, Autumn 1985.

R.L. STEVENSON (1850–1894)

308 *Collected Poems*, ed. Janet Adam Smith, London, Rupert Hart-Davis, 1950. Reprinted 1971.

The even quality of so much of Stevenson's verse came as a surprise to me when I first read it beyond the famous two or three anthology poems. Although a minor poet at the very beginnings of what became the modern Scottish Renaissance, his is a very pleasing voice. He had the potential, but lacked the will, to be great.

309 Edwin Morgan, 'The Poetry of Robert Louis Stevenson', *Scottish Literary Journal*, vol. 1, no. 2, December 1974. Printed in Morgan's *Essays*, Cheadle, Carcanet New Press, 1974 and reprinted in Morgan's *Crossing the Border*, Manchester, Carcanet, 1990. Text of the Stevenson Lecture, 1970.

JOHN DAVIDSON (1857–1909)

310 *The Poems of John Davidson*, ed. Andrew Turnbull, 2 Volumes, Edinburgh, Scottish Academic Press for the Association for Scottish Literary Studies, 1973.

311 *Poems and Ballads*, ed. Robert D. Macleod, London, Unicorn Press, 1959.

312 *John Davidson: A Selection of his Poems*, ed. Maurice Lindsay, London, Hutchinson, 1961.
Preface by T.S. Eliot. Essay by Hugh MacDiarmid. Long Introduction by Maurice Lindsay.

John Davidson's early books of poetry made him briefly famous, the collections being recognised as introducing something new into the poetry of the time, concerned with subjects that had been considered unsuitable for poetry – city squalor and the realities of life in the 1890s. Whatever fame Davidson may have had, it soon abandoned him to loneliness and neglect. Suffering from cancer he committed suicide at Penzance in 1909.

Most of Davidson's early short poems now seem very dated and of little interest to us today. The exception is his celebrated 'Thirty Bob a Week' with its use of colloquial tones within its seeming formality. T.S. Eliot acknowledged that this poem had been useful to him in his development as a poet and even in later life regarded it as 'a great poem for ever'. But Eliot also wrote that only in a very few of his lyrics had Davidson 'freed himself completely from the poetic diction of English verse of his time'. I leave short poems such as 'A Runnable Stag' and 'In Romney Marsh' to conventional anthologists.

The important poetry by Davidson, in addition to 'Thirty Bob a Week', is in his *Testaments* and in 'Crystal Palace'. The *Testaments* can be long-winded but they can also be cumulatively powerful. In his essay in 27(c) above, Edwin Morgan excellently says of Davidson's poetry that although it can be 'turgid and labyrinthine, some of it has great power of image and incident'. The *Testaments* are described by Mary O'Connor in her book, 314 below, as being 'long philosophical blank-verse poems, ranging in length from about 200 to 2000 lines'. For Hugh MacDiarmid Davidson brought scientific language and 'ideas' into poetry in a way unique in Davidson's time. Davidson could be seen as the poet of 'scientific materialism'. The most polished and controlled of the *Testaments* is *The Testament of a Man Forbid*, but the energy that is in the longer, even the more verbose, ones can be a powerful surge that gives a strength to the poetry beyond what is in the shorter ones.

Mary O'Connor indicated *Fleet Street and Other Poems*, which was posthumously published in 1909, as Davidson's 'most successful book of poems'. She points further to 'Fleet Street' and 'Crystal Palace' as major achievements by him and sees the complete 1909 volume plus 'Thirty Bob a Week' and a few other lyrics as poems in which Davidson takes his work beyond 'the category of "false starts and blind alleys" into the realm of major poetry'. I hark back to the further importance of the *Testaments* but would in no way dispute the importance of the controlled achievement that is 'Crystal Palace'. Andrew Turnbull writes in his Introduction to 310 above of this poem being Davidson's 'finest individual achievement' in the 'blank verse' of this poem. And Dr Turnbull believes this to be so not least because the poet strikes 'a balance between the informal and the mannered'. And not for the first time in Scottish poetry, much of the effect is achieved by 'the tension between colloquial and artificial elements'.

Andrew Turnbull's two-volume edition, 310 above, is a major achievement and, with its excellent notes and commentary, indispensable to a serious study of Davidson's poetry. The quantity of poems could be intimidating, however, for someone new to Davidson, but the two selected volumes I list above (nos. 311 and 312) are not adequate and we urgently need a new 'Selected Poems' of John Davidson who still awaits true recognition as a Scottish poet of considerable interest and importance.

313 J. Benjamin Townsend, *John Davidson: Poet of Armageddon*, New Haven, Yale University Press, 1961.

314 Mary O'Connor, *John Davidson*, Edinburgh, Scottish Academic Press, 1987. Scottish Writers series.

Edwin Morgan's essay, 'Scottish Poetry in the Nineteenth Century', in 27(c) above, which is reprinted in Morgan's *Crossing the Border*, Manchester, Carcanet, 1990, gives an excellent introduction to the poetry of this period and not least by highlighting the importance, even if only as minor poets, of poets of the Glasgow area. The best of these are Alexander Smith (1830–67) and David Gray (1838–61).

Alexander Smith is best known for his poem 'Glasgow'. In an essay on Smith in *Studies in Scottish Literature*, vol. 14, 1979, Mary

Jane W. Scott suggests that in 'Glasgow' the poet reveals a love-hate relationship with his city but never forgets that he belongs to it and so 'proved himself a master of that supremely Scottish talent, the poetry of realistic description'. But Smith's masterpiece goes beyond such naturalism, as does the nature poetry of James Thomson or Gavin Douglas. As I have indicated with regard to the greater poetry of Burns, this is no mere 'realism' but a re-creation into the essentially artificial that is an art form. In his essay referred to above, Edwin Morgan indicates a less well-known poem by Smith, namely 'A Boy's Poem', which is some fifty pages of poetry. Professor Morgan notes in particular 'some excellent passages reflecting love and loneliness in Glasgow and the Firth of Clyde'. See *Poetical Works of Alexander Smith*, ed. William Sinclair, Edinburgh, W.P. Nimmo, Hay & Mitchell, 1909. 'Glasgow' is printed in the anthology, *Noise and Smoky Breath. An Illustrated Anthology of Glasgow Poems 1900–1983*, ed. Hamish Whyte, Glasgow, Third Eye Centre and Glasgow District Libraries Publication Board, 1983 and there is an extract from 'A Boy's Poem' in Tom Leonard's anthology *Radical Renfrew*, no. 91 above.

The work of David Gray is mainly only an indication of potential as he died of tuberculosis at the age of twenty-one. His long descriptive poem, 'The Luggie', influenced by the eighteenth-century James Thomson, which celebrates the countryside north of Glasgow was once known to many readers, including Lanarkshire youths such as myself. Edwin Morgan, however, sees Gray's best work in a group of 'personal sonnets, owing much to Keats and Shakespeare, but delicate and moving within their limitations'. See *Poetical Works of David Gray*, ed. Henry Glasford Bell, Glasgow, Maclehose and London, Macmillan, 1874. This is a new and enlarged edition.

But for over fifty years in the nineteenth century the anthologies of popular versification entitled *Whistle-Binkie* seemed to be the pawky sentimental level to which Scottish poetry had been reduced. These volumes are recognised by Edwin Morgan as being 'carefully devised as instruments of social control'. The other side of this can be seen in the true radicalism of the poets of Renfrewshire that Tom Leonard has discovered and printed in his pioneering *Radical Renfrew: Poetry from the French Revolution to the First World War* no. 91 above.

J. Logie Robertson (1846–1922), a scholar of some repute, wrote very popular kailyird verses in Scots which were published in *The Scotsman* under the pseudonym 'Hugh Haliburton'. These poems, known as 'Hughies'!, were cut out and treasured in manses, bothies,

and schoolrooms all over Scotland. His first collection of poems was
Horace in Homespun, 1886. J. Logie Robertson, learned M.A.,
contributed preface, notes and glossary and generally acted the
patronising editor who put 'a bit of Latin at the beginning of each
sketch' and saw in 'Hughies experience of life among the hills of
Scotland a remarkable correspondence to that of Horace, twenty
centuries ago, in ancient Rome'. To such low levels had sunk the
tradition of Henryson, Dunbar and Burns by the end of the
nineteenth century.

For discerning comment on J. Logie Robertson and R.L.
Stevenson see Colin Milton's essay, 'Modern Poetry in Scots before
MacDiarmid', in 27(d) above. Many another poet of this period and
into the twentieth century is listed in my *A Bibliography of Scottish
Poets from Stevenson to 1974*, 4 above. It has an introduction which
reveals, I trust, the weaknesses of these versifiers between Stevenson
and MacDiarmid.

SECTION VIII
Twentieth-Century Poets

A. FORERUNNERS TO A RENAISSANCE

JAMES PITTENDRIGH MACGILLIVRAY (1856–1938)
315 *Pro Patria*, Edinburgh, Robert Grant, 1915.
316 *Bog-myrtle and Peat Reek*, Privately Printed by the Author for Subscribers, 1922.
The best poetry of Pittendrigh MacGillivray's *Bog-myrtle and Peat Reek* is written in a vigorous Scots and is work that asks for re-assessment. MacGillivray was never a popular poet. In this respect he is neither a Logie Robertson ('Hugh Haliburton') nor a Charles Murray (see 319 and 320 below); not even a Stevenson. He had a searching intelligence and did not exclude it from his poetry in Scots. But perhaps his lack, mostly, of sentimentality was what worked most against his achieving popularity as a Scots poet. At its exceptional best his poetry reveals a modern sensibility that truly only came into Scottish poetry with the early Scots lyrics of Hugh MacDiarmid.

VIOLET JACOB (1863–1946)
317 *The Scottish Poems of Violet Jacob*, Edinburgh, Oliver & Boyd, 1944.
This book should be reprinted or another selection made now that this pre-MacDiarmid lyrical poetry is regaining critical understanding.
318 Janet Caird, 'The Poetry of Violet Jacob and Helen B. Cruickshank', *Cencrastus*, no. 19, Winter 1984.

CHARLES MURRAY (1864–1941)
319 *Hamewith: The Complete Poems of Charles Murray*, Aberdeen, Aberdeen University Press for the Charles Murray Memorial Trust, 1979. Introduction by Nan Shepherd.
Hamewith, first published in 1900, was enlarged in 1909 and it has gone through many editions since, being one of the bestsellers of modern Scottish poetry.

87

320 *Cassette*
   Hamewith and other poems, Glasgow, Scotsoun, 1980, SSC 056.
   Charles Murray was an exile in South Africa and whilst there he
   began writing verse in his native Scots of the North-east. Many of
   his poems are heavy with the exile's nostalgic sentimentality. His
   Hamewith was first published in Aberdeen in 1900 and extended
   editions followed of what was for many years a bestseller; his poetry
   remains a favourite in the North-east. The popularity of Murray's
   poetry helped to make other work in Scots acceptable to a 'polite'
   readership after the long, long years when it had been banished to
   the world of the lower slopes of 'culture'. Stevenson's poetry in
   Scots restored some little dignity to the language and so also did
   Murray's verses. For many years Murray's most admired poem was
   'The Whistle' and others have thought highly of 'Dockens Afore His
   Peers' which, indeed, is as a dramatic monologue well suited to
   Murray's colloquial Scots. It is also as a monologue within the
   mainstream of much Scots poetry. But Alexander Scott indicated a
   better poem by Murray when he printed 'Gin I Was God' as the first
   poem of his anthology, *Voices of Our Kind*, Edinburgh, Chambers,
   1987.
      For a more extended selection from Murray's poetry, see the
   anthology *Ten Northeast Poets*, edited by Leslie W. Wheeler,
   Aberdeen, Aberdeen University Press, 1985. This anthology also
   prints work by Violet Jacob, Marion Angus and Helen B.
   Cruickshank, all of whom I list in this guide. There are also, in Mr
   Wheeler's useful book, poems by John M. Caie, Hunter Diack, Flora
   Garry, John C. Milne, David Rorie and Mary Symon, all of whom
   are important in continuing the vigorous tradition of poetry in
   Northeast Scots. For a higher rating of Murray's poetry than mine
   see Colin Milton's essay, 'From Charles Murray to Hugh
   MacDiarmid: Vernacular Revival and Scottish Renaissance',
   Literature of the North, eds. David Hewitt and Michael Spiller,
   Aberdeen, Aberdeen University Press, 1983.

MARION ANGUS (1866–1946)

321 *Selected Poems*, ed. Maurice Lindsay, with a Personal Memoir by
   Helen B. Cruickshank, Edinburgh, Serif Books, 1950.
   There is a purity of lyricism that lifts the heart, not least in the sad
   poems. Again we need a selection in print.
322 Janet Caird, 'The Poetry of Marion Angus', *Cencrastus*, no. 25, Spring
   1987.

ALEXANDER GRAY (1882–1968)

323 *Selected Poems*, ed. Maurice Lindsay, Glasgow, William Maclellan, [1948]. Poetry Scotland series.

This is a very good selection, not least for the selection from the many songs Alexander Gray translated from Heinrich Heine. There are other later books of translations of European balladry and folk song by Alexander Gray, but the poems in this selection give us his true lyric impulse. Yet again we need a selection put into print. Ten of Alexander Gray's versions of Heine's songs are included in the anthology *European Poetry in Scotland*, 88 above.

324 Alexander Scott, 'Sir Alexander Gray, 1882–1968', *Studies in Scottish Literature*, vol. 8, no. 2, October 1970.

At a somewhat greater remove from the MacDiarmid 'age' of Scottish poetry we can now see that the pure lyricism of the poetry of Violet Jacob and Marion Angus, and the rather different lyricism of Alexander Gray, was played down in the effort of several generations of poets, my own not excluded, to restore the name of 'high art' to poetry in Scots. After the long years of sub-Burnsian kailyardism and anti-intellectualism, this rejection of traditional 'local' versifiers was understandable, and even necessary to enable the Scots tradition to move into new forms and to have higher aims. Now, however, we can acknowledge that the lyricism of Violet Jacob, Marion Angus and Alexander Gray has given us a poetry to be recognised as excellent in its own terms. It is not, of course, major poetry. It is an expression of a world – both social and poetic – that has now gone, but it is a poetry true to itself in its own time.

ANDREW YOUNG (1885–1971)

325 *The Poetical Works*, ed. Edward Lowbury and Alison Young, London, Secker & Warburg, 1985.

The poetry of Andrew Young probably does not belong in this section at the beginning of the twentieth-century Scottish renaissance in poetry. This is as much a matter of form and tone in his verse as of Scottishness. To me his poetry does seem to be essentially of the English tradition and the editors of his *Poetical Works* do most obviously regard him in their Introduction as such. Nevertheless it is interesting to see, as with Drummond and many another Scottish poet who has attempted poetry in English, that Young's Scottish accent can be heard when, for example, he rhymes 'wood' with 'amplitude'. I think of Andrew Young's poems as 'charming' which is, no doubt, a poor compliment to verse that has given many readers considerable pleasure.

326 *Andrew Young, Prospect of a Poet: Essays and Tributes by Fourteen Writers*, ed. Leonard Clark, London, Hart-Davis, 1957.

327 Iain Crichton Smith, 'A Note on Andrew Young', *Lines Review*. no. 22, Winter 1966.

Iain Crichton Smith points to Scottish qualities in Young's verse, as does Tom Scott in the Introduction to his Penguin anthology, 67 above.

328 Roger D. Sell, *Trespassing Ghost: A Critical Study of Andrew Young*, Abo, Abo Akademi, 1978.

HELEN B. CRUICKSHANK (1886–1975)

329 *Collected Poems*, Edinburgh, Reprographia, 1971.

330 *More Collected Poems*, Edinburgh, Gordon Wright, 1978.

331 *Cassettes*

Helen B. Cruickshank reads from her Collected Poems, Edinburgh, Caley Recording Co., 1975. 2 tapes.

In her essay, 'Twentieth-century Women's Writing: The Nest of Singing Birds', 27(d) above, Joy Hendry writes that 'The twenty or so years between her and Jacob and Angus made an enormous difference'. Ms Hendry is referring, firstly, to the changed position of women in society, and although she was still restricted, Helen Cruickshank was able to participate 'in life on an equal basis with men'. Also, of course, in her view of the world revealed in the stances within the poetry, she is a more modern poet than Violet Jacob or Marion Angus. As Joy Hendry says, she has a greater range 'of tone and mood' than her older contemporaries although 'not such a careful craftswoman'. She has also to be seen apart from Angus or Jacob in that she has a voice which is very much her own. To group these three poets together is to fail to recognise their individual qualities as writers. In the verse of Helen B. Cruickshank there is a distinct and powerful sense of humanity that makes it still alive and important to us, which is not to underestimate the purity of the lyricism in her best poems. Her most famous poem is the superbly singing and free, in terms of attitudes to kirky morality, 'Shy Geordie' but interestingly, and most perceptively, Joy Hendry points to 'At the End' as Helen Cruickshank's most moving poem.

332 Gordon Wright, 'Helen B. Cruickshank's Fifty Years of Verse Writing', *Catalyst*, no. 2, Summer 1969.

A biographical essay with a superb photograph of Miss Cruickshank reading at the window of her home where she entertained the writers of Scotland through many generations – she was truly a 'catalyst' as Hugh MacDiarmid said.

333 Janet Caird, 'The Poetry of Violet Jacob and Helen B. Cruickshank', *Cencrastus*, no. 19, Winter 1984.

For an essay on four women writers of this generation see 'Feminine Quartet' by Marion Lochhead, *Chapman*, nos. 27/28, Summer 1980. The four writers are Violet Jacob, Marion Angus, Helen B. Cruickshank and Agnes Mure Mackenzie. The whole issue is on 'Women's contribution to twentieth-century Scottish culture'. See also Dorothy Porter's essay, 'Scotland's Songstresses', *Cencrastus*, no. 25, Spring 1987.

B. TWENTIETH-CENTURY RENAISSANCE POETS – FIRST WAVE

This is the Renaissance inspired and led by Hugh MacDiarmid, as James VI led his Renaissance in the late sixteenth century. I have already indicated similarities between the two movements at the head of Section IV above. But this twentieth-century Renaissance came after an almost total collapse of the Scottish tradition in poetry during the nineteenth century. It is for that reason a more remarkable achievement; a miracle was wrought in restoring to a distinctively Scottish poetry qualities that it had mostly lacked since Robert Burns. The essential quality is the difference between versification and a poetry that is a high art form that aims to take in all that man can aspire to, even if that can never be achieved. It is the ambition to write a poetry that is not content with being seen as a small rustic corner of a cabbage patch that is thought to be Scotland. It is a claim for an independent Scottish poetry. It is a claim for the poetry of Scotland again to be one of the poetries of Europe – and the world. But most of all it is an attempt to rise to the highest challenge that can face any poet – to achieve authentic utterance in an art form. The Scots-writing poets after Burns to the beginning of this century were of low ambition. Those who wrote in English regarded their work as belonging to English literature. The poets of this century, and especially since the twenties, have aimed for the highest – and as Scottish poets.

There is an extensive body of writing on this twentieth-century Renaissance from Hugh MacDiarmid's essays and books in the twenties right through to today.

334 Duncan Glen, *Hugh MacDiarmid (Christopher Murray Grieve) and the Scottish Renaissance*, Edinburgh, Chambers, 1964.
This book has an extensive bibliography of the poets to 1962 and of the general cultural background and history.

335 Alexander Scott, *The MacDiarmid Makars 1923–1972*, Preston, Akros Publications, 1972.

336 Robin Fulton, *Contemporary Scottish Poetry: Individuals and Contexts*, Loanhead, Macdonald Publishers, 1974.The 'Individuals' on whom there are separate essays are: Edwin Morgan, Iain Crichton Smith and Norman MacCaig. The 'Contexts' are: 'Geographical and Social', 'Private' and 'Linguistic'.

337 Alan Bold, *Modern Scottish Literature*, London, Longman, 1983.

EDWIN MUIR (1887–1959)

338 *Collected Poems*, London, Faber & Faber, 1963. Reprinted. Paperback edition 1984. This had been preceded by *Collected Poems 1921–1958*, London, Faber & Faber, 1960, which is not as complete a collection as the 1963 edition.

339 *Selected Poems*, London, Faber & Faber, 1965. Introduction by T.S. Eliot. Reprinted.

340 *Selected Letters*, ed. P.H. Butter, London, The Hogarth Press, 1974. Edwin Muir was born in Orkney but his family soon moved to Glasgow where he suffered psychologically in a most destructive way, although perhaps the poet of later years benefited from these experiences as much as from his Orkney 'Eden'. After his Glasgow years Muir became truly a citizen of Europe and a critic of world literature. He is, within the whole long length of the Scottish tradition in poetry, a major figure; one of the greatest to have written only (almost) in English. If he suffered in Glasgow in his adolescence, he suffered also in post-1945 Europe and out of that came some very fine poetry.

341 J.C. Hall, *Edwin Muir*, London, Longmans, Green for the British Council and the National Book League, 1956. Writers and their Work series.

342 Edwin Morgan, 'Edwin Muir', *The Review*, 5th February 1963. Reprinted in Edwin Morgan's *Crossing the Border*, Manchester, Carcanet, 1990.

343 P.H. Butter, *Edwin Muir: Man and Poet*, Edinburgh, Oliver & Boyd, 1966.

344 Elizabeth Huberman, *The Poetry of Edwin Muir: The Field of Good and Ill*, New York, Oxford University Press, 1971.

345 Christopher Wiseman, *Beyond the Labyrinth: A Study of Edwin Muir's Poetry*, Victoria, British Columbia, Sono Nis Press, 1978.

346 Elgin W. Mellown, *Edwin Muir*, Boston, Twayne Publishers, 1979.

347 *Lines Review*, no. 69, June 1979, has three essays on Edwin Muir.

348 Roger Knight, *Edwin Muir: An Introduction to His Work*, London, Longman, 1980.

349 *Akros*, no. 47, August 1981, is a special Edwin Muir issue.

350 *Chapman*, no. 49, Summer 1987, has a special feature on Edwin Muir.

351 James Aitchison, *The Golden Harvester: The Vision of Edwin Muir*, Aberdeen, Aberdeen University Press, 1988.

352 *Edwin Muir: Centenary Assessments*, ed. C. J. M. MacLachlan and D. S. Robb, Aberdeen, Association for Scottish Literary Studies, 1990. Ocassional Paper no. 9.
For a full bibliography of Edwin Muir to 1970 see Elgin W. Mellown, *Bibliography of the Writings of Edwin Muir*, Alabama, University of Alabama Press, 1964; revised edition, London, Nicholas Vane, 1966 and reprinted 1970.
See also Peter C. Hoy and Elgin W. Mellown, *A Checklist of Writings about Edwin Muir*, Troy, New York, Whitston, 1971.

DOMHNALL (RUADH) MAC AN T-SAOIR (DONALD MACINTYRE) (1889–1964)

353 *Sporan Dhòmhnaill: Gaelic Poems and Songs*, ed. Somerled Macmillan, Edinburgh, Oliver & Boyd for the Scottish Gaelic Texts Society, 1968.
Donald Macintyre is listed here because of the date of his birth, but he is somewhat out of place as a poet of the First Wave of poets of the modern Renaissance. He was a native of South Uist but lived for many years in Paisley, near Glasgow. He belongs to some extent within the village-verse tradition, or has some links to it; but he is a poet of a modern stance also and as such demands inclusion here as a poet of this twentieth-century Renaissance. Derick Thomson has written enthusiastically: 'In one sense it is as though one of the eighteenth-century poets had been alive in our midst in the twentieth century. Here we find the same teeming vocabulary, the same fluency in using Gaelic, the same mastery of metre. Yet in another sense the poetry is undeniably of our time, in its subject matter and in its attitudes ... The poetry has tremendous verve, wit and humour.'

HUGH MACDIARMID (CHRISTOPHER MURRAY GRIEVE) (1892–1978)

354 *Complete Poems 1920–1976*, eds. Michael Grieve and W.R. Aitken, 2 Volumes, London, Martin Brian & O'Keeffe, 1978. Paperback edition with corrections and a few additional poems as an eight-page appendix, 2 Volumes, Harmondsworth, Penguin Books, 1985. The Penguin Modern Classics.

355 *Selected Poems*, eds. David Craig and John Manson, Harmondsworth, Penguin Books, 1970. Reprinted.

356 *The Hugh MacDiarmid Anthology: Poems in Scots and English*, eds. Michael Grieve and Alexander Scott, London, Routledge & Kegan Paul, 1972. Paperback edition 1975. Reprinted.

A very good introduction to MacDiarmid's poetry, not least because it prints the complete *A Drunk Man Looks at the Thistle*.

357 *The Socialist Poems of Hugh MacDiarmid*, eds. T.S. Law and Thurso Berwick, London, Routledge & Kegan Paul, 1978.

358 *A Drunk Man Looks at the Thistle. An Annotated Edition*, ed. Kenneth Buthlay, Edinburgh, Scottish Academic Press for the Association for Scottish Literary Studies, 1987. Also paperback edition in the Scottish Classics series, 1987.

359 *The Letters of Hugh MacDiarmid*, ed. Alan Bold, London, Hamish Hamilton, 1984.

Cassettes

360 *Poems of Hugh MacDiarmid*, Selected by Kenneth Buthlay, Glasgow, Scotsoun, 1976, SSC 028, 029, 2 tapes.

LPs

361 *The Poetry of Hugh MacDiarmid*, spoken by Iain Cuthbertson and the Author, Waverley, 1962, ZLP 2007.

362 *Hugh MacDiarmid Reads His Own Poetry*, Claddagh, 1969, CCT5.

363 *A Drunk Man Looks at the Thistle: Hugh MacDiarmid Reads His Own Poem*, Claddagh, 1970, CCA 1 & 2, 2 LPs.

364 *Hugh MacDiarmid. Whaur Extremes Meet*, Tuatha, 1979, TU1.

For the first time since Robert Burns we have, in Hugh MacDiarmid, a Scottish poet who is a major writer in an international context. This is a poetry of magnificent range, from the most lyrical of short love poems to gargantuan poems that fit no classification. There is violent hatred, satire, extended flights of soaring imagination, the most complex patterns of thought matched by the emotion that motivates the thought. He is one of the great synthesisers of literature, a poet who draws in all the world of literature, language and life that is his disparate experience and makes of it a unity that remains diverse, tense and yet the conflict is resolved at the level of great poetry. As with Dunbar, his work lacks the humanity of a Burns or a Henryson, but the emotional content of the poetry is one of its strengths and works powerfully upon our imaginations, which is finally a human response. The very highest points of this great poetry are the early short lyrics in Scots: 'The Watergaw', 'The Eemis Stane', 'Empty Vessel' and 'Moonstruck' and the book-length *A Drunk Man Looks at the Thistle*, again in Scots, and as great an achievement as anything in Scottish poetry. Of the poems in English, I would indicate the longer 'On a Raised Beach'.

Hugh MacDiarmid's prose was vital in promoting the idea of a distinctively Scottish literature. For details of MacDiarmid's important prose which has been printed in book form see W.R.

Aitken's 'Selected Bibliography' in Alan Bold, *MacDiarmid: A Critical Biography*, London, John Murray, 1988. Paperback edition, London, Grafton, 1990.

365 *Hugh MacDiarmid: A Festschrift*, eds. K.D. Duval and Sydney Goodsir Smith, Edinburgh, K.D. Duval, 1962.

366 Kenneth Buthlay, *Hugh MacDiarmid (C.M. Grieve)*, Edinburgh, Oliver & Boyd, 1964. Writers and Critics series. Revised and enlarged edition, Edinburgh, Scottish Academic Press, 1982. Scottish Writers series. This remains the best single-author critical introduction to the poetry.

367 Duncan Glen, *Hugh MacDiarmid (Christopher Murray Grieve) and the Scottish Renaissance*, Edinburgh, Chambers, 1964.

368 *Agenda*, vol. 5, no. 4 – vol. 6, no. 1, Autumn-Winter 1967–8, is a double issue: Hugh MacDiarmid and Scottish Poetry.

369 *Akros*, nos. 13–14, April 1970, is a special Hugh MacDiarmid double issue.

370 *Hugh MacDiarmid: A Critical Survey*, ed. Duncan Glen, Edinburgh, Scottish Academic Press, 1972.

371 Edwin Morgan, *Hugh MacDiarmid*, Harlow, Longman for the British Council, 1976. Writers and their Work series.

372 Roderick Watson, *Hugh MacDiarmid*, Milton Keynes, Open University Press, 1976.

373 *Akros*, nos. 34–5, August 1977, is a special Hugh MacDiarmid double issue.

374 Gordon Wright, *MacDiarmid: An Illustrated Biography*, Edinburgh, Gordon Wright, 1977.

375 *The Age of MacDiarmid: Essays on Hugh MacDiarmid and His Influence on Contemporary Scotland*, eds. P.H. Scott and A.C. Davis, Edinburgh, Mainstream, 1980.

376 Anne Edwards Boutelle, *Thistle and Rose: A Study of Hugh MacDiarmid's Poetry 1920–1934*, Loanhead, Macdonald, 1981.

377 Alan Bold, *MacDiarmid: The Terrible Crystal*, London, Routledge & Kegan Paul, 1983.

378 Catherine Kerrigan, *'Whaur Extremes Meet': The Poetry of Hugh MacDiarmid 1920–1934*, Edinburgh, Mercat Press, 1983.

379 Nancy K. Gish, *Hugh MacDiarmid: The Man and His Work*, London, Macmillan, 1984.

380 Harvey Oxenhorn, *Elemental Things: The Poetry of Hugh MacDiarmid*, Edinburgh, Edinburgh University Press, 1984.

381 Roderick Watson, *MacDiarmid*, Milton Keynes, Open University Press, 1985.

382 Peter McCarey, *Hugh MacDiarmid and the Russians*, Edinburgh, Scottish Academic Press, 1987.

383 Alan Bold, *MacDiarmid: Christopher Murray Grieve: A Critical Biography*, London, John Murray, 1988. Paperback edition with corrections, London, Paladin/Grafton Books, 1990.

384 Alan Riach, *Hugh MacDiarmid's Epic Poetry*, Edinburgh, Edinburgh University Press, 1991.

For an extensive listing of MacDiarmid's books, see W.R. Aitken, 'A Hugh MacDiarmid Bibliography', *Hugh MacDiarmid: A Critical Survey*, ed. Duncan Glen, Edinburgh, Scottish Academic Press, 1972. This bibliography is continued in W.R. Aitken, 'Hugh MacDiarmid's Recent Bibliography', *Akros*, nos. 34–5, August 1977.

For a very inclusive list of writings on Hugh MacDiarmid to 1978, see Michael K. Glenday, 'Hugh MacDiarmid: A Bibliography of Criticism, 1924–78', *Bulletin of Bibliography*, vol. 36, no. 2, April–June 1979.

WILLIAM JEFFREY (1896–1946)

385 *Selected Poems*, ed. Alexander Scott, Edinburgh, Serif Books, 1951. I confess to hesitating about the poetry of William Jeffrey. In the fifties I thought very highly of two longer poems in Scots, 'The Galleys' and 'On Glaister Hill', but regarded the bulk of Jeffrey's poems in English as being of a very conventional kind. Later, for some twenty years I have also thought that his Scots poems were also of little worth. In his *Scottish Literature in English and Scots, 6* above, W.R. Aitken writes of Jeffrey, 'A poet of great sincerity and tenderness whose work shows his admiration of Blake and Yeats'. I found this an unexpected statement to read in the early eighties. Of course the lack of his own voice in English was one reason why I thought Jeffrey's poetry of little worth. But having been sent back to Jeffrey's work by Dr Aitken's words I now believe that Jeffrey is a poet whose work requires reassessment. There are ten collections of poems which preceded the 1951 volume listed above, the first being *Prometheus Returns and other poems*, London, Erskine MacDonald, 1921.

NAOMI MITCHISON (1897–)

386 *The Cleansing of the Knife and other poems*, Edinburgh, Canongate, 1978. Naomi Mitchison is best known as a novelist but her poetry requires proper critical assessment.

WILLIAM SOUTAR (1898–1943)

387 *Poems of William Soutar: A New Selection*, ed. W.R. Aitken, Edinburgh, Scottish Academic Press, 1988.

A first-rate selection, It had been preceded by another selection by W.R. Aitken, *Poems in Scots and English*, Edinburgh, Oliver & Boyd, 1961; Edinburgh, Scottish Academic Press, 1975.

Cassettes

388 *William Soutar: Scots Poems*, Selected by Alexander Scott, Glasgow, Scotsoun, SSC 026.

389 *William Soutar: Poems, Riddles, Song*, Glasgow, Scotsoun, SSC 033.

390 *William Soutar: Merry Matanzie*, Glasgow, Scotsoun, 1989. SSC 083. Alex McCrindle reads his own selection of thirty-seven poems by Soutar. Comment by W.R. Aitken and a Memoir by Alex Galloway which is read by W.R. Aitken.

William Soutar is a poet who is in many ways a traditionalist in his verse forms. Within these accepted limitations he wrote, at his best, poetry which revealed no trace of a parochial mind. This is poetry that has links with the lyrical work of Burns, and earlier poets also, but it belongs without qualification in the world of twentieth-century poetry. There are few of the grand and fearlessly innovative features in Soutar's poetry that mark that of Hugh MacDiarmid, but it is a poetry of significance in showing that the traditional Scots forms could be extended by a poet of some considerable talent. We can now see that William Soutar was the only poet of the twenties and thirties writing in Scots who could learn much from MacDiarmid while retaining an independent voice.

Although outside the strict limits of this book, I would refer readers to Soutar's prose, most of which is unpublished. Alexander Scott edited a selection from Soutar's Diaries and there are extracts from his Journals in *Scottish Review*, no. 10, 1978, and in *Chapman*, no. 53, Summer 1988. The selection that Scott edited was published as *Diaries of a Dying Man*, Edinburgh, Chambers, 1954, new reprint 1988. This is a moving testament to the courage, intelligence, humanity and generosity of spirit of Soutar who was bedridden for much of his adult life.

Hugh MacDiarmid edited *Collected Poems*, London, Andrew Dakars, 1948, but it is a botched job, omitting many of Soutar's best poems in Scots, although it did make available much previously unpublished work.

391 Alexander Scott, *Still Life: William Soutar (1898–1943)*, Edinburgh, Chambers, 1958.

392 George Bruce, *William Soutar (1898–1943): The Man and the Poet: An Essay*, Edinburgh, National Library of Scotland, 1978.

393 George Bruce, 'The Poetry of William Soutar: Reasoning Man, Intuitive Poet', *Akros*, no. 43, April 1980.

394 *Chapman*, no. 53, Summer 1988, is a William Soutar number.

The poets of Maurice Lindsay's first edition of his anthology, *Modern Scottish Poetry*, 1946, 82 above, whom I do not list either as forerunners or in this First Wave of the Renaissance, or who do not seem to me to belong to the Second Wave, of which Maurice Lindsay's own poetry was a part, are: John Ferguson, Hamish MacLaren, Albert Mackie, Margot Robert Adamson, Donald Sinclair, Lewis Spence and Muriel Stuart. If we turn to the MacQueen/Scott Oxford anthology, 66 above, we can add the following poets: Edith Anne Robertson, Bessie J.B. MacArthur, Margaret Winefride Simpson, Joe Corrie, Robert Rendall and Alice V. Stuart. I believe that the poetry of Lewis Spence (1874–1955), who wrote his best work in Scots, and of Donald Sinclair (1886–1933), who wrote in Gaelic, will be re-assessed to reveal a few poems of some worth. See *Collected Poems of Lewis Spence*, Edinburgh, Serif Books, 1953. Sinclair's poetry remains uncollected. Muriel Stuart [Irwin], (1885–1967) would have a separate listing in this book but as Margery McCulloch argues most convincingly in a pioneering essay, there is little justification for continuing to regard Muriel Stuart as a Scottish poet and 'certainly none for claiming her as a participant in the Scottish Literary Renaissance movement of the early 1920s'. For Dr McCulloch's essay entitled 'Muriel Stuart: A Cuckoo in the Nest of Singing Birds?' see *Scottish Literary Journal*, vol. 16, no. 1, May 1989. Whether of the Scottish tradition or not, this is a fine poet. Her collections of poetry include: *The Cockpit of Idols*, London, Methuen, 1918; *Poems*, London, Heinemann, 1922; and *Selected Poems*, London, Cape, 1927.

C. TWENTIETH-CENTURY RENAISSANCE POETS – SECOND AND THIRD WAVES

AONGHAS CAIMBEUL (1903–82)

395 *Moll is Cruithneachd*, Glaschu, Gairm, 1972.

The nickname of Aonghas Caimbeul was Am Puilean and the translation of the title of his book, above, is 'Chaff and Wheat'. He is a poet of humour and satire, committed to his own twentieth-century environments, including a Polish prison-camp during the 1939–45 war. But he is also secure, in other poems, within the tradition of village verse and within the linguistically rich Gaelic tradition.

396 Roy G. Wentworth, 'Bàrdachd Aonghais Chaimbeil (Am Puilean)' ('The Poetry of Angus Campbell (the Puilean)'), *Gairm*, 138, Spring 1987.

FORBES MACGREGOR (1904–)

397 *Four Gates of Lothian and other poems 1921–1978*, ed. Alastair Mackie, Edinburgh, Forbes Macgregor, 1979.

Forbes Macgregor began writing powerful poetry in the twenties and has continued to do so to this day. A man who has the courage of his belief in strong, vigorous and sometimes earthy Scots. His wit matches his technical control.

WILLIAM MONTGOMERIE (1904–)

398 *From Time to Time: Selected Poems*, Edinburgh, Canongate, 1985.

William Montgomerie published two books of poetry in the thirties but, although known through publication in magazines and anthologies, the full range and his total achievement were not truly revealed until the publication of the above book in 1985.

399 Edwin Morgan, 'A Note on William Montgomerie', *Chapman*, no. 46, Winter 1986–7.

400 Duncan Glen, 'William and Norah Montgomerie', *Scottish Poetry Library Newsletter*, no. 10, New Year, 1987.

J.K. ANNAND (1908–)

401 *Wale o Rhymes*, Edinburgh, Macdonald, 1989.

A selection of bairn rhymes from three separate collections.

402 *Two Voices*, Edinburgh, Macdonald, 1968.

403 *Poems and Translations*, Preston, Akros Publications, 1975.

404 *Cassette*

Aince for Pleisure and Twice for Joy, Glasgow, Scotsoun, 1976, SSC 009.

A selection of bairn rhymes.

J.K. Annand is best known for his bairn rhymes which have enjoyed wide success since the publication of *Sing it Aince for Pleisure* in 1965. Two other collections followed and now we have the admirable selection from them listed above. His other two collections of poetry which are not bairn rhymes reveal that he has been writing poetry since the twenties when, as a pupil at Broughton School, he first corresponded with Hugh MacDiarmid.

405 Janet Campbell, 'The Bairn Rhymes of J.K. Annand', *Akros*, no. 26, December 1974.

DERIC BOLTON (1908–)

406 *A View from Ben More and other poems*, Walton-on-Thames, Outposts Publications, 1972.

407 *Glasgow Central Station*, Walton-on-Thames, Outposts Publications, 1972.

408 *The Wild Uncharted Country*, Walton-on-Thames, Outposts Publications, 1973.

409 *Grown Over with Green-ness*, Walton-on-Thames, Outposts Publications, 1976.

Deric Bolton is a research chemist as well as a poet and he can make excellent use of his scientific viewpoint in his poetry. His poem 'My Uncle Eustace, Maker of Rings', published in *Nature* in 1977, has been described as 'probably the definitive poem in English *by* a scientist *about* a scientist'.

GEORGE BRUCE (1909–)

410 *The Collected Poems of George Bruce*, Edinburgh, Edinburgh University Press, 1971.

411 *Perspectives: Poems 1970–1986*, Aberdeen, Aberdeen University Press, 1987.

George Bruce is a poet with a very individual voice. It is a spare yet highly emotive poetry, utterly Scottish and yet showing that he had learned much that was of use to him from Ezra Pound and William Carlos Williams in the thirties.

412 Alexander Scott, 'Myth-Maker: The Poetry of George Bruce', *Akros*, no. 29, December 1975.

413 Iain Crichton Smith, '*Sea Talk* by George Bruce' in Crichton Smith's *Towards the Human*, Loanhead, Macdonald, 1986.

OLIVE FRASER (1909–77)

414 *The Wrong Music. The Poems of Olive Fraser, 1909–1977*, ed. Helena M. Shire, Edinburgh, Canongate, 1989.

Yet another poet who has been unjustly ignored by critics. Although the importance of her work is in its gentleness it has strengths that grow in the mind; the lyricism is uncluttered and sings admirably within a considerable range.

ROBERT GARIOCH (1909–81)

415 *George Buchanan, 'Jephthah' and 'The Baptist': Translatit frae Latin in Scots*, Edinburgh, Oliver & Boyd, 1959.

The translator's name on the title-page is Robert Garioch Sutherland.

416 *Complete Poetical Works*, ed. Robin Fulton, Loanhead, Macdonald, 1983.

See also *A Robert Garioch Miscellany*, ed. Robin Fulton, Edinburgh, Macdonald, 1986, which prints 'The Masque of Edinburgh', some reviews by Garioch and some of his letters, or extracts from them. There are also essays on Garioch's poetry and on the man.

417 *Cassette*
   Poems, selected by Edwin Morgan, Glasgow, Scotsoun, 1978, SSC
   045.
   If Robert Fergusson was the Villon of Edinburgh in the eighteenth
   century, then Robert Garioch is the Giuseppe Belli of Edinburgh in
   the twentieth. Garioch's translations from the Roman 'dialect' of
   Belli into Scots are one of the major achievements of this century in
   any form of creative work. I believe them to be Garioch's finest
   achievement. A large group of these Belli sonnets are in the
   France/Glen anthology, 88 above. The Roman poet gave Garioch a
   courage in the translations that he lacked in his original poetry. But
   that is to ask something of Robert Garioch which would have
   lessened one of his strengths – the sense in the poetry of his dread,
   his awareness of the horror of life. So for all the success of his comic
   verse as vital humour, it is the underlying sense of that hatred of
   what the world does to humankind that gives it an important extra
   dimension. It is this that gives meaning to his longer, and seemingly
   more serious, poems, but as so often the greatest tragic view of
   reality is in the so-called comic.

418 D.M. Black, 'Poets of the Sixties – III: Robert Garioch', *Lines Review*,
   no. 23, Spring 1967.

419 Roderick Watson, 'The Speaker in the Gairdens: The Poetry of
   Robert Garioch', *Akros*, no. 16, April 1971.

420 Donald Campbell, 'Another Side to Robert Garioch, Or, A Glisk of
   Near-Forgotten Hell', *Akros*, no. 33, April 1977.

421 *Chapman*, no. 31, Winter 1981/82, has three essays by way of being
   an 'In Memoriam: Robert Garioch' by David Black, J.K. Annand and
   Derek Bowman.

422 Don W. Nichol, 'Belli Up To Date: Scots and English Sonnet
   Translations by Robert Garioch and Anthony Burgess', *Chapman*,
   no. 39, Autumn 1984.

423 Iain Crichton Smith, 'The Power of Craftsmanship: The Poetry of
   Robert Garioch' in Crichton Smith's *Towards the Human*, Loanhead,
   Macdonald, 1986.

DOUGLAS FRASER (1910–)

424 *Rhymes o' Auld Reekie*, Loanhead, Macdonald Publishers, 1973.

425 *Where the Dark Branches Part: A Sequence of Love Poems*, Loanhead,
   Macdonald, 1977.

426 *Treasure for Eyes to Hold*, Kinnesswood, Lomond Press, 1981.
   Douglas Fraser has wider range than his well-known Edinburgh
   rhymes would suggest.

NORMAN MACCAIG (1910–)

427 *Collected Poems, New Edition*, London, Chatto & Windus, 1990.
Supersedes edition of 1985 printing poems of *Voice-Over*, 1988 and
also fifteen new poems written since.

Norman MacCaig's poetry reveals yet again that a new rhythm is
a new reality. I say this to emphasise that for all the power of what
are the most sophisticated and truly enjoyable philosophical and
metaphysical 'conceits' perhaps in the whole range of Scottish
poetry, finally it is their marriage to the powerful yet seemingly
easily achieved rhythms that makes this important poetry. A poetry
of intelligent wit coming from a mind that is intellectual and sardonic
yet finally very human in its awareness of not only the world out
there but that within the poet's own head making his own world that
in the words of Jack Rillie, 'takes the skin off its own self-conceit'.

428 *Cassette*
Nineteen Poems of Norman MacCaig, Glasgow, Association for Scottish
literary Studies in co-operation with Scotsoun, SSC 306. Commentary
by Edwin Morgan with readings by Norman MacCaig.

429 *LP*
The Way I Say It: Poems, Claddagh, 1973, CCA4.

430 Iain Crichton Smith, 'The Poetry of Norman MacCaig', *Saltire
Review*, no. 19, 1959.

431 *Akros*, no. 7, March 1968, is a Norman MacCaig issue.

432 W.S. Porter, 'The Poetry of Norman MacCaig', *Akros*, no. 32,
December 1976.

433 Erik Frykman, '*Unemphatic Marvels*': A Study of Norman MacCaig's
Poetry, Gothenburg, University of Gothenburg, 1977.

434 *Chapman*, no. 45, Summer 1986 has a 'Special Feature on Norman
MacCaig'.

435 Raymond Ross, 'Norman MacCaig: The History Man', *Cencrastus*,
no. 33, Spring 1989.

436 Roderick Watson, *The Poetry of Norman MacCaig*, Aberdeen,
Association for Scottish Literary Studies, 1989. Scotnotes no. 5.

437 *Norman MacCaig: Critical Essays*, ed. Joy Hendry and Raymond
Ross, Edinburgh, Edinburgh University Press, 1990.
Modern Scottish Writers series.

438 *Scottish Poetry Library Newsletter*, no. 16, January 1991 has essays on
MacCaig by Brian McCabe and Colin Nicholson.
See also 336 above.

SOMHAIRLE MACGILL-EAIN (SORLEY MACLEAN) (1911–)

439 *O Choille gu Bearradh. From Wood to Ridge. Collected Poems in Gaelic
and English*, Manchester, Carcanet, 1989.

Parallel text with MacLean's own translation.

440 *Reothairt is Contraigh: Taghadh de Dhàin 1932–72. Spring Tide and Neap Tide: Selected Poems 1932–72*, Edinburgh, Canongate, 1977. Latest paperback edition, 1988.

441 *Cassette*
14 Poems of Sorley MacLean, Glasgow, Association for Scottish Literary Studies in collaboration with Scotsoun, 1986, SSC 304. Commentary by Iain Crichton Smith with readings by Sorley MacLean.

442 *LP*
Barran agus Asbhuain. Claddagh, 1973, CCA3.
Poems read by the poet. A booklet gives bilingual texts.
In the poetry of Donald Macintyre (see 353 above) and Aonghas Caimbeul (see 395 above), we have a reworking mainly of older-type Gaelic poetry, sometimes with the village poet attitudes, although both of these poets do venture into a poetry of the twentieth century in various ways. With the poetry of Sorley MacLean we enter a quite new world of poetry. This is a revolution in the tradition; it is the first statement of a true twentieth-century Gaelic poetry. It is major poetry and has been recognised as such in the last ten or so years around the world. The discerning minority recognised the greatness of this poetry in 1943 with the publication of MacLean's *Dàin do Eimhir agus Dàin Eile* in Glasgow by William Maclellan.

In his essay 'Modern Gaelic Poetry', *Akros*, no. 6, December 1967 (reprinted in 58 above), Iain Crichton Smith writes of *Dain do Eimhir* as 'the greatest Gaelic book of this century'. He writes of 'Glac a' Bhàis' ('Death Valley'), 'In this poem we have the formal power and justice of the Greeks'. And in the same essay Mr Smith also writes, 'His greatest poem in my opinion is "Hallaig"; a strange moving poem not amenable to the reason but emerging, I believe, from a racial consciousness uncorrupted by the strategies of the mind.'

443 J. A. MacDonald, 'The Work of Sorley MacLean', *Jabberwock*, vol. 3, no. 2, April 1950.

444 *Somhairle MacGill-Eain/Sorley MacLean*, Edinburgh, National Library of Scotland, 1981.
An exhibition at the Library, July–November 1981. Introduction by William Gillies.

445 John MacInnes, 'A Radically Traditional Voice: Sorley MacLean and the Evangelical Background', *Cencrastus*, no. 7, Winter 1981–82.

446 *Sorley MacLean: Critical Essays*, eds. Raymond J. Ross and Joy Hendry, Edinburgh, Scottish Academic press, 1986.

447 Colin Nicholson, 'Poetry of Displacement: Sorley MacLean and his Writing', *Studies in Scottish Literature*, vol. 22, 1987.

448 Iain Crichton Smith, 'Gaelic Master: Sorley MacLean', *Scottish Review*, no. 34, May 1984. Reprinted in Crichton Smith's *Towards the Human*, Loanhead, Macdonald, 1986.

449 Christopher Whyte, 'The Cohesion of 'Dàin do Eimhir'', *Scottish Literary Journal*, vol. 17, no. 1, May 1990.

J.F. HENDRY (1912–86)

450 *The Bombed Happiness*, London, Routledge, 1942.

451 *Marimarusa*, Thurso, Caithness Books, 1978.

452 *A World Alien*, Dunfermline, Borderline Press, 1980.
     A fine poet who awaits critical recognition.

453 *Chapman*, no. 52, Spring 1988, is 'On J.F. Hendry'.

SYDNEY TREMAYNE (1912–86)

454 *Selected and New Poems*, London, Chatto & Windus, 1973.
     A quiet but beautiful poetry.

455 George Bruce, 'The Poetry of Sydney Tremayne', *Akros*, no. 38, August 1978.

JANET CAIRD (1913–)

456 *Some Walk a Narrow Path*, Edinburgh, The Ramsay Head Press, 1977.

457 *A Distant Urn*, Edinburgh, The Ramsay Head Press, 1983.

458 *John Donne, You Were Wrong*, Edinburgh, Ramsay Head Press, 1988.

DOUGLAS YOUNG (1913–73)

459 *Auntran Blads: An Outwale o Verses*, Glasgow, Maclellan, 1943.

460 *A Braird o Thristles: Scots Poems*, Glasgow, Maclellan, 1947. Poetry Scotland series.

461 *A Clear Voice: Douglas Young, Poet and Polymath*, [ed. Clara Young and David Murison], Loanhead, Macdonald, 1977.
     A selection from his writings, with a memoir and a bibliography. Douglas Young's poetry is written in a Scots that makes no concessions to any anglicisation of the Scots language, being what in 1989 can be termed neo-baroque. Much of this, as with others who believe that they have to establish the separateness of their Scots from English, is mostly a matter of spelling, which can be useful in indicating pronunciation. But I refer to this to indicate that his poetry is not as artificial as it may look to those not familiar with this style of spelling, or unable to project what is on the page into sounds. Currently Young's poetry is out of fashion; time will enable

others to judge it. For certain, however, some of his poems will live on in anthologies. And so also will his magnificent translation of Paul Valéry's 'Le Cimetière Marin', included in the France/Glen anthology, 88 above.

R. CROMBIE SAUNDERS (1914–91)

462 *The Year's Green Edge and other poems*, Killin, Crombie Saunders, [1987].
463 *This One Tree*, Killin, Crombie Saunders, [1987].
   A stylish poet who has not been given his critical due. He published two books of poetry in the fifties but 462 above collects poems from them.

IAN BOWMAN (1915–87)

464 *Orientations: Selected Poems*, Preston, Akros Publications, 1977.
   Ian Bowman is perhaps at his best as a poet in the poems in Scots relating to mining, but his range is varied in both Scots and English.

G.S. FRASER (1915–80)

465 *Poems*, eds. Ian Fletcher and John Lucas, Leicester, Leicester University Press, 1981.
   An exiled Scot whose sensitive and technically very sure-footed poetry is much wider in scope than the often-printed anthology pieces by which he is best known would suggest. The man's humanity radiates from his poetry.
466 Patrick Scott, 'G.S. Fraser', *Cencrastus*, no. 16, Spring 1984.

DEORSA CAIMBEUL HAY (GEORGE CAMPBELL HAY) (1915–84)

467 *Fuaran Sléibh. Rainn Ghàidhlig*, Glasgow, Maclellan, 1948.
468 *Wind on Loch Fyne*, Edinburgh, Oliver & Boyd, 1948.
469 *O Na Ceithir Airdean*, Edinburgh, Oliver & Boyd, 1952.
470 *Four Points of a Saltire: The Poetry of Sorley MacLean, George Campbell Hay, William Neill, Stuart MacGregor*, Edinburgh, Reprographia, 1970.
471 *Mochtàr is Dùghall*, Glaschu, Roinn nan Cànan Ceilteach, Oilthigh Ghlaschu, 1982.
   George Campbell Hay's 1948 book, *Fuaran Sléibh*, was published, as was Sorley MacLean's masterpiece, *Dàin do Eimhir*, by William Maclellan. It is the second collection of Gaelic poetry of major significance in revealing a renaissance of Gaelic poetry in this century. But Hay wrote poetry in all three languages of Scotland. Now that his poetry, and even more so that of Sorley MacLean, is

so much admired it is easy to forget how neglected it was until the publication of *Four Points of a Saltire*, 470 above, began the wider appreciation of this important poetry. Reprographia is an earlier imprint of Gordon Wright. But it was not until 1980, when Angus Martin discovered it, that Hay's *Mochtàr is Dùghall* was even known to exist although it was written in the 1940s. This epic, although unfinished, comprises over 1,200 lines. See Ronald I.M. Black's essay, 'Thunder, Renaissance and Flowers: Gaelic Poetry in the Twentieth Century' in 27(d) above, where he describes this poem as 'one of the great sustained achievements of Gaelic literature'. A 'Collected Poems' of George Campbell Hay is being edited.

472 William Neill, 'The Poetry of George Campbell Hay', *Scotia Review*, no. 8, December 1974.

473 Iain Crichton Smith, 'George Campbell Hay: Language at Large', *Scottish Review*, no. 35, August 1984. Reprinted in Crichton Smith's *Towards the Human*, Loanhead, Macdonald, 1986.

474 Derick S. Thomson, 'George Campbell Hay: A Tribute', *Scottish Review*, no. 35, August 1984.

475 Donald E. Meek, 'Land and Loyalty: The Gaelic Verse of George Campbell Hay', *Chapman*, no. 39, Autumn 1984.

476 Robert A. Rankin, 'George Campbell Hay As I Knew Him', *Chapman*, no. 40, Spring 1985.

477 William Gillies, 'Deòrsa Caimbeul Hay', *Gairm*, nos. 135 and 136, Summer and Autumn 1986.

SYDNEY GOODSIR SMITH (1915–75)

478 *Collected Poems 1941–1975*, London, John Calder, 1975.

479 *Cassette*
     Under the Eildon Tree: A Poem in XXIV Elegies, Glasgow, Scotsoun, 1977, SSC 024.

480 *LP*
     Deevil's Waltz: Sydney Goodsir Smith reads his poetry, Claddagh, 1978, CCA8.

Sydney Goodsir Smith's long poem, *Under the Eildon Tree*, is unquestionably one of the great poems of twentieth-century Scottish literature. It is wild and abandoned at one level but in fact superbly organised and controlled within its seeming freedom. It is not the poem that a cautious poet could have written; Goodsir Smith risked everything and pulled it off brilliantly. His short lyrics, including some very fine love lyrics, are in severe contrast to his extended sequence. Another major poem is 'The Grace of God and the Meth-Drinker', in an elevated language of extremes that could have broken out of controlled wildness to fall to the floor where most such extravagances of language end in forgettable failure. But the structure holds, and we have a masterpiece.

481 Norman MacCaig, 'The Poetry of Sydney Goodsir Smith', *Saltire Review*, vol. 1, no. 1, April 1954.

482 *Akros*, no. 10, May 1969, is a Sydney Goodsir Smith issue.

483 Thomas Crawford, 'The Poetry of Sydney Goodsir Smith', *Studies in Scottish Literature*, vol. 7, nos. 1 and 2, July–October 1969.

484 *Scotia Review*, no. 9, April 1975, is a Sydney Goodsir Smith memorial issue.

485 *For Sydney Goodsir Smith*, Loanhead, M. Macdonald, 1975.
A memorial volume. It is mainly biographical and critical essays by various writers.

486 Eric Gold, *Sydney Goodsir Smith's 'Under the Eildon Tree': An Essay*, Preston, Akros Publications, 1975.

487 Kenneth Buthlay, 'Sydney Goodsir Smith: Makar Macironical', *Akros*, no. 31, August 1976.

488 Thom Nairn, 'A Route Maist Devious: Sydney Goodsir Smith and Edinburgh', *Cencrastus*, no. 33, Spring 1989.

T.S. LAW (1916–)

489 *Whit Tyme in the Day*, Glasgow, Caledonian Press, 1948.

490 *Referendum*, Blackford, Fingerpost Publications, 1989.
Prints poems from three earlier collections published between 1974 and 1980 and some other later poems. Many other poems remain uncollected including some very, very long poems written in the eighties.

Referendum reveals, as the author correctly says in his 'Foreword', 'a pettren o Scottish natiounalist thochtiness' which was going on in Scotland in the years when the poems were written. But they are also poems that project into what goes beyond politics.

W.S. GRAHAM (1918–86)

491 *Collected Poems 1942–1977*, London, Faber & Faber, 1979.

492 *Uncollected Poems*, London, Greville Press, 1990.
At one time Graham was seen as a 'difficult' poet whose poetry seemed to lack logical structure and to make imaginative jumps that readers could not follow. This is indeed a poetry that is complex in its linguistic and 'thought' patterns but we now more easily accept such constructions and Graham's poetry is now widely recognised as a major achievement.

493 William Montgomerie, 'The Novelty of Language: The Poetry of W.S. Graham', *Lines Review*, no. 10, December 1955.

494 Robert Duxbury, 'The Poetry of W.S. Graham', *Akros*, no. 38, August 1978.

495 Edwin Morgan, 'The Sea, the Desert, the City: Environment and Language in W.S. Graham, Hamish Henderson, and Tom Leonard', *The Yearbook of English Studies*, vol. 17, ed. C.J. Rawson, Modern Humanities Research Association, 1987. Reprinted in Morgan's *Crossing the Border*, Manchester, Carcanet, 1990.

496 *Edinburgh Review*, no. 75, 1987, has a long section on the life and work of W.S. Graham.

497 Tony Lopez, *The Poetry of W.S. Graham*, Edinburgh, Edinburgh University Press, 1989.
This has a very full bibliography.

MAURICE LINDSAY (1918–)

498 *Collected Poems 1940–1990*, Aberdeen, Aberdeen University Press, 1990.
Supersedes *Collected Poems*, 1979 and prints poems from collections published between 1981 and 1988 and includes some 'final revisions' as well as some recent unpublished poems.
As many another critic has written, this is poetry which gives true pleasure. It is easily under-estimated because of its ease of reading whther it be lyrical or satirical poems.

499 Donald Campbell, 'A Different Way of Being Right: The Poetry of Maurice Lindsay', *Akros*, no. 24, April 1974.

500 Lorn M. Macintyre, 'The Poetry of Maurice Lindsay', *Akros*, no. 42, December 1979.

501 Christopher Rush, 'Maurice Lindsay's *Collected Poems*', *Scottish Literary Journal*, Supplement no. 12, Spring 1980.

TOM SCOTT (1918–)

502 *An Ode til New Jerusalem*, Edinburgh, M. Macdonald, 1956.

503 *The Ship and ither poems*, London, Oxford University Press, 1963. This volume includes three very fine translations of poems by Villon: 'Ballat o the Appeal', 'Ballat o the Leddies o Langsyne' and 'Ballat o the Hingit'; they are reprinted in the France/Glen anthology, 88 above. These and other translations were printed in Tom Scott's earlier book, *Seeven Poems o Maister Villon*, Tunbridge Wells, The Pound Press, 1953.

504 *At the Shrine o the Unkent Sodger. A Poem for Recitation*, Preston, Akros Publications, 1968.

505 *Brand the Builder*, Epping, Ember Press, 1975.

506 *The Tree: An Animal Fable*, Dunfermline, Borderline Press, 1977.

507 *The Dirty Business: A Poem About War*, Barr, Ayrshire, The Blew Blanket Library, Luath Press, 1986.

508 *Views from Myeloma (excerpts 17 and 18)*, Child Okeford, Words Press, 1988. Mir Poets 19.

In his own terms, Tom Scott is a 'bard', a public poet rather than one of personal 'confession'; a commentator on society and politics, especially on war, see 504 and 507 above. His finest achievement is *Brand the Builder*.

509 John Herdman, 'Towards New Jerusalem, The Poetry of Tom Scott', *Akros*, no. 16, April 1971.

510 Thomas Crawford, 'Tom Scott: From Apocalypse to Brand', *Akros*, no. 31, August 1976.

511 *Scotia Review*, nos. 13 and 14, August-November 1976. A Tom Scott double issue.

512 J. Derrick McClure, 'The Versification of Tom Scott's *The Tree*', *Scottish Literary Journal*, Supplement no. 10, Summer 1979.

513 *Chapman*, nos. 47–8, Spring 1987, has a special feature on Tom Scott.

WILLIAM J. TAIT (1918–)

514 *A Day Between Weathers: Collected Poems 1938–1978*, Edinburgh, Paul Harris, 1980.

William J. Tait is at his very best in the Scots of his native Shetland, revealing that such a poetry can be both local and European.

HAMISH HENDERSON (1919–)

515 *Elegies for the Dead in Cyrenaica*, London, John Lehmann, 1948. Second edition, Edinburgh, Edinburgh University Student Publications Board, 1977. Latest edition, Edinburgh, Polygon, 1990.

516 LP

Freedom Come All Ye: The Poems and Songs of Hamish Henderson, Claddagh Records, 1977, CCA7.

In print Hamish Henderson is currently a poet of one book, but his *Elegies* is a major achievement. Equally important are his songs which are sung around the world. See (and hear in the above LP) also the superb extract from the unpublished poem, 'The Roses of Edinburgh', on the Meadows of Edinburgh, which moves most effectively through varying levels of tone and language. The text of this extract, entitled 'Floret Silva Undique', is printed in the booklet which accompanies the LP listed above. It is also in Robin Bell's anthology, *The Best of Scottish Poetry*, 89 above, as is Hamish Henderson's 'Freedom Come-All-Ye' which is one of the finest Scottish songs being, like so many that have survived, not only song but also a high art creation. The insert with the LP prints the text of 'Freedom Come-All-Ye' and other famous songs; it also has a good introduction by Thomas Crawford.

517 *Chapbook*, vol. 3, no. 6, [1965], is a special issue on Hamish Henderson. In addition to essays on his life and work, this number of this famous folk magazine also prints the text and music of seven songs with most useful accompanying commentary.

518 Jack Mitchell, 'Hamish Henderson and the Scottish Tradition', *Calgacus*, vol. 1, no. 3, Spring 1976. A revised version of an essay first published in 1965.

519 Richard E. Ziegfeld, 'The Elegies of Rilke and Henderson: Influence and Variation', *Studies in Scottish Liteature*, vol. 16, 1981.

520 *Chapman*, no. 42, Winter 1985, is, in part, a Hamish Henderson number.

521 Andrew R. Hunter, 'Hamish Henderson: The Odyssey of a Wandering King', *Aberdeen University Review*, no. 178, Autumn 1987.

522 Duncan Glen, 'Hamish Henderson: Poetry becomes People', *Inter-Arts*, vol. 1, no. 7, October 1988.
See also no. 495 above.

DOMHNALL IAIN MACDHOMHNAILL (DONALD JOHN MACDONALD) (1919–86)

523 *Sguaban Eòrna*, Inbhir Nis, Club Leabhar, 1974.

EDWIN MORGAN (1920–)

524 *Collected Poems*, Manchester, Carcanet, 1990.
Supersedes *Poems of Thirty Years*, 1982. Prints some fifty uncollected and unpublished poems ranging in date from 1939 to 1990.

525 *Rites of Passage: Selected Translations*, Cheadle, Carcanet Press, 1976. For translations by Edwin Morgan which add to these unique and important ones, see the France/Glen anthology, 88 above, but even these additional poems do not reveal the full extent of Morgan's work as a translator.

526 *Selected Poems*, Manchester, Carcanet Press, 1985. Poetry Signatures series.

527 *Cassette*
Seventeen Poems of Edwin Morgan, Glasgow, Association for Scottish Literary Studies in co-operation with Scotsoun, 1986, SSC 305. Commentary by Roderick Watson and readings by Edwin Morgan.

528 *LP*
A Double Scotch: Edwin Morgan and Alexander Scott read their own poetry, Claddagh, 1971, CCA5.

The range of Edwin Morgan's poetry is quite remarkable. It takes in not only his native Glasgow but also outer space, and in form and technique ranges from quite formal verbal structures to concrete poetry, which is of course also, in its own way, formal. Indeed, as the title of one of his books affirms, it is 'From Glasgow to Saturn' in language and form as well as in geography. And as with all true poetry, that geography is both real and unreal, as its time is unconfined by chronology, taking in as it does past, present and future. On the sleeve of the LP listed above, Norman MacCaig writes well on one of his contemporaries, 'while most poets write about the past as well as the present, he writes about the future as well as the present – space-age poems, a sort of science-fiction poetry. I used to find something forced about all this and would sometimes mutter to myself that there are few things more out of date than being up to date. But I have changed my mind. Morgan clearly *is* a man of this moment. This is no act. He does not wobble on a bandwagon but stands solid in his true self. And his observations, meditations, narratives – even his jokes – are made into true poems by his affection and compassion for his fellow creatures. This means that in spite of his delight in experimenting, even playing, with words, his poetry is fundamentally a social poetry. The necessary ego of the poet is never obtrusive. Nothing "confessional" here.'

529   Robin Hamilton, 'The Poetry of Edwin Morgan', *Akros*, no. 43, April 1980. Reprinted with minor alterations in Hamilton's *Science and Psychodrama: The Poetry of Edwin Morgan and David Black*, Frome, Bran's Head Books, 1982.

530   Kenneth White, 'Morgan's Range', *Cencrastus*, no. 12, Spring 1983.

531   Walter Perrie, 'Edwin Morgan', *Chapman*, no. 37, Autumn 1983.

532   Geddes Thomson, *The Poetry of Edwin Morgan*, Aberdeen, Association for Scottish Literary Studies, 1986. Scotnotes no. 2.

533   *About Edwin Morgan*, ed. Robert Crawford and Hamish Whyte, Edinburgh, Edinburgh University Press, 1990. Modern Scottish Writers series. Includes 'Edwin Morgan: A Checklist' compiled by Hamish Whyte which comprises 115 most valuable pages.

534   *Nothing Not Giving Messages: Reflections on the Life and Work of Edwin Morgan*, ed. Hamish Whyte, Edinburgh, Polygon, 1990.
      Morgan on his life and work through interviews.

535   Hamish Whyte and Robert Crawford, 'Morgan Matters', *Scottish Poetry Library Newsletter*, no. 15, August 1990.

536   *Cencrastus*, no. 38, Winter 1990/91 is an Edwin Morgan special issue.
      See also 336 above.

ALEXANDER SCOTT (1920–89)

537 *Selected Poems 1943-1974*, Preston, Akros Publications, 1975.

Cassettes

538 *Poems in Scots*, Glasgow, Scotsoun, 1978, SSC 044.

539 *A Bonnie Fechter: Alexander Scott 1920–1989*, Glasgow, Scotsoun, 1990, SSC 086.

540 *LP*

A Double Scotch: Edwin Morgan and Alexander Scott read their own poetry, Claddagh, 1971, CCA5.

The language and tone of Alexander Scott's poetry have often been described as not only powerful but aggressive. For contemporaries to write on a poet's work can be vital in giving a useful insight into the work for future generations. Sometimes the response is so confined by the literary politics of the day that a contemporary critic cannot see beyond such politics, or beyond the man he knew. But when a contemporary gets it right it is superb. And no one more so than Norman MacCaig as his essay on Morgan which I quoted from above reveals as does a review by him of Alexander Scott's *Cantrips*, 1968, in *Akros*, no. 9, January 1969. I quote a few sentences to show qualities that Dr MacCaig saw in the poems when he wrote on the second part of Scott's poem 'To Mourn Jayne Mansfield'. 'Scott's sympathy with the lamentable deaths of these two ladies [Jayne Mansfield and Marilyn Monroe] is nowhere explicit. It lies behind the harsh directness of the statements and the apparent brutality of the humour. But it's there. It's made available (to me at least) by the *tone* of the poem, which is related to the very Scottish habit of disguising a true affection behind an outspoken coarseness which I myself have seen bamboozling interested foreigners . . . unless one is responsive to the sympathy, the tenderness, behind their [some of Scott's poems] crusty exterior one is going to make, in my view, a very wrong judgment of them.'

541 J.K. Annand, 'Alexander Scott: an Introduction', *Akros*, no. 16, August 1971.

542 George Bruce, 'The Poetry of Alexander Scott', *Akros*, no. 19, August 1972.

543 Lorn Macintyre, 'Alexander Scott, Makar Extraordinary', *Akros*, no. 25, August 1974.

544 Leonard Mason, *Two North-East Makars: Alexander Scott and Alastair Mackie*, Preston, Akros Publications, 1975.

545 Ruth Lennox, 'The Poetry of Alexander Scott', *Akros*, no. 33, April 1977.

546 Duncan Glen, 'Alexander Scott', *Scottish Poetry Library Newsletter*, no. 14, February 1990.

GEORGE MACKAY BROWN (1921–)

547 *Selected Poems*, London, The Hogarth Press, 1977.

548 *Voyages*, London, Chatto & Windus/The Hogarth Press, 1983.

549 *The Wreck of the Archangel*, London, John Murray, 1989.

550 LP
George Mackay Brown: the Orcadian Poet reads his poems and a story, Claddagh, 1971, CCA6.

George Mackay Brown is as much a creative prose writer as a poet but there is a unity in all his writings. In his work we have a voice unique in modern literature. This is not only because of his particular Orcadian view of the world, of reality – it is a matter of personal forms. But he *is* influenced by the Scandinavian inflences on the culture of Orkney. But he has also seen the Gaelic element – his mother was a Gaelic speaker from Sutherland – as being equally important. On the sleeve of the LP listed above he writes, 'Intricate pattern; a sense of the numinous pervading the world of "getting and spending"; the contrast of enduring stone with spindrift and blossom and breath – my work is touched here and there, I think, with these Celtic attitudes'. He sees himself trying to suggest, 'the swift dangerous rhythms of the sea, and (even more important) the slow fruitful rhythm of the earth from seedtime to harvest. (one of my books of verse is called *Loaves and Fishes* and a later one *Fishermen with Ploughs*)'.

551 Stewart Conn, 'Poets of the Sixties –II: George Mackay Brown', *Lines Review*, no. 22, Winter 1966.

552 Douglas Dunn, ' "Finished Fragrance": The Poems of George Mackay Brown', *Poetry Nation*, no. 2, 1974.

553 Philip Pacey, 'The Fire of Images: The Poetry of George Mackay Brown', *Akros*, no. 32, December 1976. Reprinted in Philip Pacey's *David Jones and Other Wonder Voyagers: Essays*, Bridgend, Poetry Wales Press, 1982.

554 *Chapman*, no. 60, Spring 1990 includes a Special Feature on George Mackay Brown.

RUARAIDH MACTHOMAIS (DERICK THOMSON) (1921–)

555 *Creachadh na Clàrsaich. Plundering the Harp. Collected Poems 1940-1980*, Edinburgh, Macdonald, 1982.

This extensive collection includes twenty-three previously uncollected poems.

If the poetry of Sorley MacLean and George Campbell Hay was quickly recognised by discerning readers as a poetry that had created with impressive rapidity a renaissance of Gaelic poetry, the publication of the first volume of Derick Thomson's poetry, *An Dealbh Briste*, in 1951, reassured many that that renaissance was not to be a two-poet one. Thomson writes a modern, socially involved poetry without a hint of parochialism or excessive looking back either in subject-matter or in his forms. That would be expected of a man of Thomson's learning, but what is important is that he speaks as a poet absorbing his knowledge, building on it and taking off from that into what cannot be constructed by cold reason – quite simply, into the statement that can be said only in poetry. Ronald I.M. Black writes of Derick Thomson in 27(d) above, 'his is the major voice of Gaelic poetry in the second half of the twentieth century'.

556 Donald MacAulay, 'Introduction', *Lines Review*, no. 39, December 1971. An essay on Thomson's poetry in this number which is devoted to his poetry, Gaelic with English versions by the poet himself.

557 John MacInnes, 'The World through Gaelic-Scots Eyes', *Lines Review*, no. 85, June 1983.

558 Christopher Whyte, 'Derick Thomson: Reluctant Symbolist', *Chapman*, no. 38, Spring 1984.

559 Iain Crichton Smith, 'The Poetry of Derick Thomson', *Scottish Review*, no. 37, February–May, 1985. Reprinted in Crichton Smith's *Towards the Human*, Loanhead, Macdonald, 1986.

560 Fearghas MacFhionnlaigh, 'Borbhan Comair – Ath-sgrùdadh air Bàrdachd Ruaraidh MhicThòmais' ('Tumbling of Burns in Confluence – a Re-assessment of the Poetry of Derick Thomson'), *Gairm*, no. 131, Summer 1985.

WILLIAM NEILL (UILLEAM NEILL) (1922–)

561 *Scotland's Castle*, Edinburgh, Reprographia, 1969.

562 *Four Points of a Saltire: The Poetry of Sorley MacLean, George Campbell Hay, William Neill, Stuart MacGregor*, Edinburgh, Reprographia, 1970.

563 *Despatches Home*, Edinburgh, Reprographia, 1972.

564 *Galloway Landscape and other poems*, Haugh of Urr, Urr Publications, 1981.

565 *Cnù à Mogaill*, Glaschu, Roinn nan Canan Ceilteach, Oilthigh Ghlaschu, 1983.

566 *Wild Places: Poems in Three Leids*, Barr, Luath Press, 1985.

567 *Blossom, Berry, Fall and Selected Work*, Gatehouse, Heart Boox, 1986. The selected work edited by Roderick MacQueen.

568 *Making Tracks and other poems*, Edinburgh, Gordon Wright Publishing, 1988.

G.F. DUTTON (1924–)

569 *31 Poems*, Oxford, Anne Stevenson, 1977. Old Fire Station Poets 1.
570 *Camp One*, Edinburgh, Macdonald, 1978. Lines Review Edition series no. 7.
571 *Squaring the Waves*, Newcastle-upon-Tyne, Bloodaxe Books, 1986.

KEN MORRICE (1924–)

572 *Prototype*, Edinburgh, M. Macdonald, 1965.
573 *Twal Mile Roon: Poetry of Aberdeen and the North-East*, Dyce, Rainbow Books, 1985.
This book prints some poems from *Relations*, 1979 and *For All I Know*, 1981.
574 *When Truth is Known*, Aberdeen, Aberdeen University Press, 1986.
575 George Bruce, 'The Poetry of Ken Morrice', *Aberdeen University Review*, no. 178, Autumn 1987.

IAN HAMILTON FINLAY (1925–)

576 *The Dancers Inherit the Party: Selected Poems*, Worcester, England and Ventura, Calif., Migrant, 1960. Reprinted.
577 *Glasgow beasts, an a burd, haw, an inseks, an, aw, a fush*, Edinburgh, Wild Flounder Press, [1961]. Reprinted.
A pioneering poem in the Glasgow dialect which is reprinted in *Noise and Smoky Breath: An Illustrated Anthology of Glasgow Poems 1900–1983*, ed. Hamish Whyte, Glasgow, Third Eye Centre and Glasgow District Libraries Publications Board, 1983. Reprinted.
578 *Poems to Hear and See*, New York, the Macmillan Co., London, Collier-Macmillan, 1971.
Ian Hamilton Finlay has an international reputation for his visual poetry and other printed visual works, and for his sculpture. In a letter, *The Guardian*, 18th April 1988, Alasdair Gray describes Ian Hamilton Finlay as 'Scotland's only landscape poet' and writes of enjoying 'the flowerbeds, pools, twining paths and sculptures of Little Sparta, Mr Finlay's home near Biggar'. But the two books of poems listed above, first published in 1960 and 1961, are also important and have been far more influential than has been acknowledged.
579 Yves Abrioux, *Ian Hamilton Finlay: A Visual Primer*, with Introductory Notes and Commentaries by Stephen Bann, Edinburgh, Reaktion Books, 1985. A joy to look at, but also an excellent scholarly book with very good notes, references and a most extensive bibliography which not only lists Finlay's many works but also leads into the many other writings on his work.
580 *Cencrastus*, no. 22, Winter 1986, has an Ian Hamilton Finlay

'Retrospective'. Edwin Morgan's essay, 'Early Finlay' is reprinted in *Crossing the Border*, Manchester, Carcanet, 1990.

There is an extensive bibliography of Ian Hamilton Finlay's many booklets, broadsheets, cards, etc. to 1974 in Duncan Glen, *Bibliography of Scottish Poets from Stevenson to 1974*, Preston, Akros Publications, 1974.

ALASTAIR MACKIE (1925–)

581 *Back-Green Odyssey and other poems*, Aberdeen, Rainbow Books, 1980.

582 *Ingaitherins: Selected Poems*, Aberdeen, Aberdeen University Press, 1987.

The two books listed above are 'Selected Poems' and the second includes some fine early poems, but neither prints enough poems from *Clytach*, Preston, Akros Publications, 1972, which contains Alastair Mackie's finest poetry.

583 Leonard Mason, *Two North-East Makars: Alexander Scott and Alastair Mackie*, Preston, Akros Publications, 1975.

584 George Bruce, 'The Poetry of Alastair Mackie, or Feet on the Grun', *Akros*, no. 33, April 1977.

ALASTAIR REID (1926–)

585 *Oddments, Inklings, Omens, Moments*, poems, London, Dent, 1960.

586 *Weathering: Poems and Translations*, Edinburgh, Canongate, 1978.

NORMAN KREITMAN (1927–)

587 *Touching Rock*, Aberdeen, Aberdeen University Press, 1987.

588 *Against the Leviathan*, Aberdeen, Aberdeen University Press, 1989.

BURNS SINGER (1928–64)

589 *The Collected Poems of Burns Singer*. ed. W.A.S. Keir, London, Secker & Warburg, 1970.

590 *Selected Poems*, ed. Anne Cluysenaar, Manchester, Carcanet Press, 1977.

Burns Singer's early death has been described as the greatest loss to Scottish poetry this century.

IAIN CRICHTON SMITH (IAIN MAC A' GHOBHAINN) (1928–)

591 *Bùrn is Aran*, Glasgow, Gairm Publications, 1960.

592 *Biobuill is Sanasan-reice*, Glasgow, Gairm Publications, 1965.

593 *Rabhdan is Rudan*, Glaschu, Gairm, 1973.

594 *Eadar Fealla-dhà is Glaschu: Orain Stòlda is Orain Eibhinn*, Glaschu, Roinn nan Cànan Ceilteach, Oilthigh Ghlaschu, 1974.

595 *Selected Poems 1955–1980*, ed. Robin Fulton, Loanhead, Macdonald, 1981.

596 *Na h-Eilthirich*, Glaschu, Roinn nan Cànan Ceilteach, Oilthigh Ghlaschu, 1983.

597 *Selected Poems*, Manchester, Carcanet Press, 1985. Poetry Signatures series.
A good but less extensive selection than 588 above, but with sixteen additional, presumably later, poems.

598 *The Exiles*, Manchester, Carcanet Press, Dublin, Raven Arts Press, 1984.

599 *A Life*, Manchester, Carcanet Press, 1986.

600 *An t-Eilean agus an Cànan: Dà Ruith-dhàn*, Glaschu, Roinn nan Cànan Ceilteach, Oilthigh Ghlaschu, 1987.

601 *The Village and other poems*, Manchester, Carcanet Press, 1989.

602 *Fifteen poems of Iain Crichton Smith*, Glasgow, Association for Scottish Literary Studies Commentary 11, 1987.
Since Iain Crichton Smith published his first volume of poems, *The Long River*, in 1955, he has been recognised as one of the most accomplished of modern Scottish poets. He writes as well in English as in Gaelic, his mother tongue, and seems to have no problems over which language to choose for a particular poem. His strength as a poet, however, is that he continually sees complications in life that must be challenged and questioned.

603 Edwin Morgan, 'The Raging and the Grace: Some Notes on the Poetry of Iain Crichton Smith', *Lines Review*, no. 21, Summer 1965. Reprinted in *Essays*, Cheadle, Carcanet Press, 1974.

604 Frederic Lindsay, 'Disputed Angels: The Poetry of Iain Crichton Smith', *Akros*, no. 36, December 1977.

605 John Blackburn, *A Writer's Journey: A Study of the Poetry of Iain Crichton Smith*, Edinburgh, SCET Production for the Scottish Curriculum Development Service, 1981. Accompanied by a set of 5 cassette tapes.

606 J.H. Alexander, 'The English Poetry of Iain Crichton Smith', *Literature of the North*, eds. David Hewitt and Michael Spiller, Aberdeen, Aberdeen University Press, 1983.

607 Carol Gow, 'An Interview with Iain Crichton Smith', *Scottish Literary Journal*, vol. 17, no. 2, November 1990. Recorded in August 1987. See also 336 above.

To draw a clear dividing line between the second and third waves of twentieth-century Renaissance poets is, of course, not possible and so this break is quite arbitrary. Having indicated above poets of the first wave who are included in the first edition of Maurice

Lindsay's anthology, *Modern Scottish Poetry*, 1946, to whom I have not given a separate listing, I would do so also for those in the anthology of the second wave. These are 'Adam Drinan' (Joseph MacLeod) (1903–84), Robert Maclellan (1907–85) who is important as a playwright, Ruthven Todd (1914–78) and Donald Macrae (1921–). None of these poets has been excluded from the revised editions of Dr Lindsay's anthology: second edition, London, Faber & Faber, 1966; third edition, Manchester, Carcanet Press, 1976; and fourth edition, London, Robert Hale, 1986. If we turn to the John MacQueen/Tom Scott anthology, *The Oxford Book of Scottish Verse*, first published in 1966 as poets of the third wave were about to be recognised, there are in that anthology the following second wave poets to whom I do not give a separate listing: Norman Cameron (1905–53), Kathleen Raine (1908–), T.A. Robertson ('Vagaland') (1909–73), and 'Thurso Berwick' (Morris Blythman) (1919–82). Norman Cameron, whose *Collected Poems and Selected Translations*, eds. Warren Hope and Jonathan Barker was published, London, Anvil Press Poetry, 1990, is a poet who has tended to be ignored by many Scottish critics and his work should be reassessed although this may not alter received opinion that only a few poems are worthy of our attention; these would include, 'Public House Confidence, 'The Firm of Happiness Limited', a fine war poem 'Green, Green is El Aghir' and 'Forgive Me, Sire', the excellent four lines of which are in the MacQueen/Scott anthology although the other Cameron poems are not well chosen. Cameron worked in advertising and thought up the idea of 'Night Starvation' to advertise Horlicks. Kathleen Raine is an important poet but, despite her reported statements that she regards herself as a Scottish poet, I continue to regard her as an English one. I would, however, refer readers to her *Collected Poems 1935–1980*, London, George Allen & Unwin, 1981 and to her *Presence: Poems 1984–87*, Ipswich, Golgonoonzo Press, 1987.

Here I would also indicate two third-wave Renaissance poets who have poems in the third and fourth editions of Maurice Lindsay's *Modern Scottish Poetry* and to whom I have not given a separate listing: Anne B. Murray (1932–) and Giles Gordon (1940–) the latter being better known as a novelist.

A recent anthology of contemporary Scottish poetry is *The Best of Scottish Poetry*, edited by Robin Bell, 89 above. I would indicate poets with work included in it who have not been referred to in this guide. These are: Elma Mitchell (1919–), Eddie Linden (1935–), Alan Spence (1947–), and Stephen Scobie (1943–). An even more recent anthology is *Twenty of the Best*, edited by Duncan Glen, no. 90

above, which prints twenty-one poets who are not in no. 89 above. Poets who are in this anthology but who have not been referred to in this guide are: Matthew Fitt (1968–), Ellie McDonald (1937–) and Maureen Macnaughtan (1945–).

GAEL TURNBULL (1928–)

608 *Gathering of Poems 1950–1980*, London, Anvil Press Poetry, 1983. 609 *A Year and a Day*, Glasgow, Mariscat, 1985. 610 *From the Language of the Heart*, Kentucky, Gnomon Press, 1985. 611 *A Winter Journey*, Durham, Pig Press, 1987. 612 Kenneth Cox, 'Gael Turnbull's Poetry', *Scripsi*, vol. 2, no. 1, 1984.

MARGARET GILLIES BROWN (1929–)

613 *Give Me the Hill-Run Boys*, Walton-on-Thames, Outposts Publications, 1978.

614 *The Voice in the Marshes*, Walton-on-Thames, Outposts Publications, 1979.

615 *Hares on the Horizon*, Walton-on-Thames, Outposts Publications, 1981.

616 *No Promises: Poems*, Nottingham, Akros Publications, 1984.

617 *Looking Towards Light*, Dundee, Blind Serpent Press, 1988.

STANLEY ROGER GREEN (1929–)

618 *Advice to Travellers: Selected Poems*, Aberdeen, Aberdeen University Press, 1990.

ALASTAIR FOWLER (1930–)

619 *Catacomb Suburb*, Edinburgh, Edinburgh University Press, 1976.

620 *From the Domain of Arnheim*, London, Secker & Warburg, 1982.

DOMHNALL MACAMHLAIGH (DONALD MACAULAY) (1930–)

621 *Seòbhrach ás a' Chlaich: ceithir fichead dàn 7 eile*, Glasgow, Gairm, 1967.

622 Iain Crichton Smith, 'An Dotair Leóinte: Bárdachd Dhòmhnaill MhicAmhlaigh' ('The Wounded Doctor: the Poetry of Donald MacAulay'), *Gairm*, no. 125, Winter 1983–84.

A translation (title altered) is reprinted in Crichton Smith's *Towards the Human*, Loanhead, Macdonald, 1986.

TOM BUCHAN (1931–)

623 *Dolphins at Cochin*, London, Barrie & Rockliff, The Cresset Press, 1969.

624 *Poems 1969–1972,* Edinburgh, The Poni Press, 1972.
625 *Forwords,* Glasgow, Glasgow Print Studio, 1977.

A.D. FOOTE (1931–)

626 *The House Not Right in the Head,* Dundee, Blind Serpent Press, 1986.

GEORGE MACBETH (1932–)

627 *Collected Poems 1958–1982,* London, Hutchison, 1989.
Includes nothing from 628 below and other longer sequences are also not represented.
628 *Anatomy of a Divorce,* London, Hutchinson, 1988.
629 David M. Black, 'The Poetry of George MacBeth', *Scottish International,* no. 3, August 1968.

DUNCAN GLEN (1933–)

630 *In Appearances,* Preston, Akros Publications, 1971.
631 *Mr & Mrs J. L. Stoddart at Home,* Preston, Akros Publications, 1975.
632 *Gaitherings: Poems in Scots,* Preston, Akros Publications, 1977.
Reprints poems of three earlier collections but none of them is listed above.
633 *Realities Poems,* Nottingham, Akros Publications, 1980.
634 *On Midsummer Evenin Merriest of Nichts?,* Nottingham, Akros Publications, 1981.
635 *The Turn of the Earth,* Nottingham, Akros Publications, 1985.
636 *Tales to be Told,* Edinburgh, Akros Publications, 1987.
637 *Sometimes Edinburgh,* Edinburgh, Akros Editions, 1991.
638 Leonard Mason, *Two Younger Poets: Duncan Glen and Donald Campbell. A Study of Their Scots Poetry,* Preston, Akros Publications, 1976.
639 Philip Pacey, 'The Poetry of Duncan Glen, or Lallans and Heich Places', *Akros,* no. 33, April 1977.

ALASDAIR GRAY (1934–)

640 *Old Negatives: Four Verse Sequences,* London, Cape, 1989.

DONNCHADH MACLEOID (DUNCAN MACLEOD) (1934–)

641 *Casan Rùisgte,* Glaschu, Roinn nan Cànan Ceilteach, Oilthigh Ghlaschu, 1985.

STEWART CONN (1936–)

642 *In the Kibble Palace: New & Selected Poems,* Newcastle- upon-Tyne, Bloodaxe Books, 1987.

Includes twenty-nine new poems in addition to a well-judged selection from his five previous collections.

643 George Bruce, 'Bound by Necessity: The Poetry of Stewart Conn', *Akros*, no. 40, April 1979.

644 Iain Crichton Smith, 'Towards the Human: The Poetry of Stewart Conn', *New Edinburgh Review*, no. 62, Summer 1983. Reprinted in Crichton Smith's *Towards the Human*, Loanhead, Macdonald, 1986.

WILLIAM MCILVANNEY (1936–)

645 *In Through the Head*, Edinburgh, Mainstream, 1988.
A selection of poems from two earlier books with some new poems.

KENNETH WHITE (1936–)

646 *The Bird Path: Collected Longer Poems*, Edinburgh, Mainstream, 1989.

647 *Handbook for the Diamond Country: Collected Shorter Poems 1960–1990*, Edinburgh, Mainstream, 1990.

648 *Chapman*, no. 59, January 1989 is in part a Kenneth White issue.

ROBIN FULTON (1937–)

649 *Selected Poems 1963-1978*, Loanhead, Macdonald, 1980.

650 *Fields of Focus*, London, Anvil Press Poetry, 1982.

651 *Coming Down to Earth and Spring is Soon*, London/Plymouth, Oasis/Shearsman Books, 1990.

652 George Bruce, 'The Poetry of Robin Fulton: Clinical Poet', *Akros*, no. 41, August 1979.

RAYNE MACKINNON (1937–)

653 *The Spark of Joy and other poems*, Thurso, John Humphries, 1970.

654 *The Hitch-hiker and other poems*, Walton-on-Thames, Outposts Publications, 1976.

655 *The Blasting of Billy P. and other poems*, London, Enitharmon, 1978.

656 *Northern Elegies*, Edinburgh, The Netherbow Arts Centre, 1986.

JAMES AITCHISON (1938–)

657 *Sounds Before Sleep*, London, Chatto & Windus/The Hogarth Press, 1971. The Phoenix Living Poets series.

658 *Spheres*, London, Chatto & Windus/The Hogarth Press, 1975. The Phoenix Living Poets series.

659 *Second Nature*, Aberdeen, Aberdeen University Press, 1990.

ALAN JACKSON (1938–)

660 *Salutations: Collected Poems 1960-1989*, Edinburgh, Polygon, 1990.

STEPHEN MULRINE (1938–)

661 *Poems*, Preston, Akros Publications, 1971. Parklands Poets series no. 10.

JAMES RANKIN (1939–)

662 *Poems*, Preston, Akros Publications, 1969. Parklands Poets series no. 4.

TESSA RANSFORD (TESSA STIVEN) (1938–)

663 *Light of the Mind: Selected Poems*, Edinburgh, Ramsay Head Press, 1980.

664 *Fools and Angels*, Edinburgh, Ramsay Head Press, 1984.

665 *Shadows from the Greater Hill*, Edinburgh, Ramsay Head Press, 1987.

666 *A Dancing Innocence*, Edinburgh, Macdonald, 1988. Lines Review Editions series.

667 T[h]om Nairn, 'A Profile of Tessa Ransford', *Cencrastus*, no. 25, Spring 1987.

DONALD CAMPBELL (1940–)

668 *Selected Poems 1970–1990*, Edinburgh, Galliard, 1990.

669 Leonard Mason, *Two Younger Poets: Duncan Glen and Donald Campbell. A Study of Their Scots Poetry*, Preston, Akros Publications, 1976.

670 Frederic Lindsay, 'The Poetry of Donald Campbell', *Akros*, no. 43, April 1980.

DAVID BLACK (1941–)

671 *Collected Poems 1964-1987*, Edinburgh, Polygon, 1991.

672 John Herdman, 'The World of D.M. Black', *Scottish International*, no. 13, February 1971.

673 Robin Hamilton, 'The Poetry of David Black', *Akros*, no. 39, December 1978. Reprinted with minor alterations in Robin Hamilton's *Science and Psychodrama: The Poetry of Edwin Morgan and David Black*, Frome, Bran's Head Books, 1982.

DAVID MORRISON (1941–)

674 *The Constant Tide: Selected Poems*, Wick, Pulteney Press, 1986.

675 *Grape and Grain*, Wick, Pulteney Press, 1988.

DOUGLAS DUNN (1942–)

676 *Selected Poems 1964-1983*, London, Faber & Faber, 1986. Reprinted.

677 *Northlight*, London, Faber & Faber, 1988.

678 Robert Duxbury, 'The Poetry of Douglas Dunn', *Akros*, no. 41, August 1979.

AONGHAS MACNEACAIL (1942–)

679 *Imaginary Wounds*, Glasgow, Print Studio Press, 1980.

680 *Sireadh Bradain Sicir. Seeking Wise Salmon*, Nairn, Balnain Books, 1983.

681 *An Cathadh Mór. The Great Snowbattle*, Nairn, Balnain Books, 1984.

682 *An Seachnadh agus dàin eile. The Avoiding and other poems*, Edinburgh, Macdonald Publishers, 1986. Lines Review Editions series.

683 *Rock and Water and other poems in English*, Edinburgh, Polygon, 1990.

JENNY ROBERTSON (1942–)

684 *Beyond the Border*, Blackford, Chapman, 1989. Chapman New Writing series, no.3.

JOHN PURSER (1942–)

685 *The Counting Stick*, Breakish, Isle of Skye, Aquila Poetry, 1976.

686 *A Share of the Wind*, Portree, Isle of Skye, Aquila, 1980. Aquila Pamphlet Poetry, second series.

687 *Amoretti*, Portree, Isle of Skye, Aquila, 1985.

ALAN BOLD (1943–)

688 *In This Corner: Selected Poems 1963–1983*, Edinburgh, Macdonald, 1983.

Prints twenty-three new or uncollected poems but omits Bold's poems in Scots; 689 below prints a selection of these.

689 *Summmoned by Knox: Poems in Scots*, Paisley, Wilfion Books, 1985.

690 Douglas Dunn, 'The Poetry of Alan Bold: Hammering on the Lyre', *Akros*, no. 42, December 1979.

RODERICK WATSON (1943–)

691 *Poems*, Preston, Akros Publications, 1970. Parklands Poets series no. 7.

692 *True History on the Walls*, Loanhead, M. Macdonald, 1976. Lines Review Editions series no. 6.

IAN ABBOT (1944–1989)

693 *Avoiding the Gods*, Blackford, Chapman, 1988. Chapman New Writing series.

694 Alexander Hutchison, William Montgomerie and Colin Nicholson, 'Three Appreciations', *Scottish Poetry Library Newsletter*, no. 14, February 1990.

MAOILIOS M. CAIMBEUL (MYLES CAMPBELL) (1944–)

695 *Eileanan*, Glaschu, Roinn nan Cànan Ceilteach, Oilthigh Ghlaschu, 1980.

696 *Bailtean. Villages/Towns. Poems in Gaelic with English Versions*, Glaschu, Gairm, 1987.
697 *A' Càradh an Rathaid/Ag Cóiriu an Róid*, Dublin, Coiscéim, 1988.

THOMAS A. CLARK (1944–)

698 *Down and Out in Tighnabruaich*, Preston, Akros Publications, 1970
699 *Madder Lake*, Toronto, Coach House Press, 1981.
700 *The Homecoming*, Kenilworth, Prest Roots Press, 1988.

ALEXANDER HUTCHISON (1944–)

701 *Deep-tap Tree*, Amherst, University of Massachusetts Press, 1978.
702 *The Moon Calf*, Edinburgh, Galliard, 1990.

TOM LEONARD (1944–)

703 *Intimate Voices: Selected Work 1965–1983*, Newcastle upon Tyne, Galloping Dog Press, 1984. Reprinted.
704 *Situations Theoretical and Contemporary*, Newcastle upon Tyne, Galloping Dog Press, 1986.
705 *Nora's Place*, Newcastle-upon-Tyne, Galloping Dog Press, 1990.
706 Tom McGrath, 'Tom Leonard: Man with Two Heads', *Akros*, no. 24, April 1974.
See also Edwin Morgan, 'Glasgow Speech in Recent Scottish Literature' in *Scotland and the Lowland Tongue*, ed. J. Derrick McClure, Aberdeen, Aberdeen University Press, 1983. Reprinted in *Crossing the Border*, Manchester, Carcanet, 1990.
See also no. 495 above.

CHRISTOPHER RUSH (1944–)

707 *A Resurrection of a Kind*, Aberdeen, Aberdeen University Press, 1984.

ROBIN BELL (1945–)

708 *Sawing Logs*, London, Workshop Press, 1980.
709 *Strathinver: A Portrait Album 1945–1953*, Edinburgh, Macdonald, 1984.
710 *Radio Poems*, Calstock, Peterloo Poets, 1989.

ROBIN MUNRO (1946–)

711 *The Land of the Mind*, London, Dent, 1975.

SHEENA BLACKHALL (1947–)

712 *The Cyard's Kist and other poems*, Aberdeen, Rainbow Books, 1984.
713 *The Spik o' the Lan'*, Aberdeen, Rainbow Enterprises, 1986.
714 *Hame-drauchtit*, Aberdeen, Rainbow Books, 1987.

715 *File Doo Black Crow*, Aberdeen, Keith Murray Publications, 1989.

WILLIAM FINDLAY (1947–)
716 *Poems*, Preston, Akros Publications, 1975. Parkland Poets series no. 12.

ROBIN HAMILTON (1947–)
717 *The Lost Jockey: Collected Poems 1966–1982*, Frome, Bran's Head Books, 1985.

LIZ LOCHHEAD (1947–)
718 *Dreaming Frankenstein and Collected Poems*, Edinburgh, Polygon Books, 1984.
719 *True Confessions and New Cliches*, Edinburgh, Polygon Books, 1985. Described in the blurb as a collection of raps, songs, sketches and monologues from plays and reviews.

CATRIONA NICGUMARAID (CATRIONA MONTGOMERY) (1947–)
720 (With Mórag NicGumaraid (Morag Montgomery) (1950–) *A' Choille Chiar*, Glaschu, Clò-beag, 1974.
721 *Rè na h-Oidhche/Through the Night*, Glasgow, Dog & Bone, 1991. Bilingual text.

VALERIE GILLIES (1948–)
722 *Each Bright Eye: Selected Poems 1971–1976*, Edinburgh, Canongate, 1977.
723 *Bed of Stone*, Edinburgh, Canongate, 1984.
724 *The Chanter's Tune*, Edinburgh, Canongate, 1990.

FEARGHAS MACFHIONNLAIGH (1948–)
725 *A' Mheanbhchuileag*, Glaschu, Gairm, 1980. There is a translation by the author into English, 'The Midge', *Cencrastus*, no. 10, Autumn 1987.

RONALD BUTLIN (1949–)
726 *Creatures Tamed by Cruelty: Poems in English and Scots and Translations*, Edinburgh, Edinburgh University Student Publications Board, 1979.
727 *Ragtime in Unfamiliar Bars*, London, Secker & Warburg, 1985.
728 Colin Nicholson, ' "Widdershins This Life o Mine"': Ron Butlin's Writing', *Cencrastus*, no. 24, Autumn 1986.

WALTER PERRIE (1949–)
729 *Poem on a Winter Night*, Loanhead, Macdonald Publishers, 1976.

730 *A Lamentation for the Children*, Edinburgh, Canongate, 1977.
731 *Surge Aquilo*, Preston, Akros Publications, 1977.
732 *By Moon and Sun*, Edinburgh, Canongate, 1980.
733 *Out of Conflict*, Dunfermline, Borderline, 1982.
734 *Concerning the Dragon*, Edinburgh, Black Pennell, 1984.

DONALD GOODBRAND SAUNDERS (1949–)
735 *Findrinny: Poems*, Glasgow, Dog & Bone, 1990.

HARVEY HOLTON (1949–)
736 *Finn*, Cambridge, Three Tygers Press, 1987.
737 (With John Brewster (1957–), William Hershaw (1957–) and Tom Hubbard (1950–), *Four Fife Poets: Fower Brigs ti a Kinrik*, Aberdeen, Aberdeen University Press, 1988.

CATHERINE LUCY CZERKAWSKA (1950–)
738 *The Book of Men and other Poems*, Preston, Akros Publications, 1976.

TOM POW (1950–)
739 *Rough Seas*, Edinburgh, Canongate, 1987.
740 *The Moth Trap*, Edinburgh, Canongate, 1990.

RAYMOND VETTESE (1950–)
741 *The Richt Noise and ither poems*, Edinburgh, Macdonald Publishers, 1988. Lines Review Editions series.

ANDREW GREIG (1951–)
742 *Men on Ice*, Edinburgh, Canongate, 1977.
743 *Surviving Passages*, Edinburgh, Canongate, 1982.
744 (With Kathleen Jamie) *A Flame in Your Heart*, Newcastle upon Tyne, Bloodaxe Books, 1986.
745 *The Order of the Day*, Newcastle-upon-Tyne, Bloodaxe Books, 1990.

FRANK KUPPNER (1951–)
746 *A Bad Day for the Sung Dynasty*, Manchester, Carcanet Press, 1984.
747 *The Intelligent Observation of Naked Women*, Manchester, Carcanet Press, 1987.

BRIAN MCCABE (1951–)
748 *One Atom to Another*, Edinburgh, Polygon, 1987.
Some of the poems appeared in *Spring's Witch*, Glasgow, Mariscat Press, 1985.

GERALD MANGAN (1951–)
749 *Waiting for the Storm*, Newcastle-uon-Tyne, Bloodaxe Books, 1990.

JOHN GLENDAY (1952–)
750 *The Apple Ghost*, Calstock, Peterloo Poets, 1989.

COLIN MACKAY (1952–)
751 *Red Ice*, Chapman, 1987. Chapman New Writing series.

ANGUS MARTIN (1952–)
752 *The Larch Plantation*, Edinburgh, Macdonald, 1990. Lines Review
Editions series.

PETE FAULKNER (1953–)
753 *Rats Dance by Candlelight*, Breakish, Skye, Aquila Publishing, 1976.
754 *Reptile Fun: Poems 1977–1979*, Dundee, The Author, [1984].

ANDREW FOX (1953–)
755 *Darkness and Snowfall*, Carnoustie, Blind Serpent Press, 1989.

DILYS ROSE (1954–)
756 *Madame Doubtfire's Dilemma*, Blackford, Chapman, 1989. Chapman
New Writing series.
Some of the poems had appeared in *Beauty is a Dangerous Thing*,
[Edinburgh], Top Copy, 1988.

HUGH MCMILLAN (1955–)
757 *Tramontana: Poems*, Glasgow, Dog & Bone, 1990.

MAIRI NICGUMARAID (MARY MONTGOMERY) (1955–)
758 *Eadar Mi 's a' Bhreug*, Dublin, Coiscéim, 1988.
There is a parallel translation in Irish.

GEORGE GUNN (1956–)
759 *The Reinstating of Skins*, Wick, Pulteney Press, 1977.
760 *Explaining to Joni*, Edinburgh, Dwarick Press, 1979.
761 *The Winter-House*, Thurso, Caithness Press, 1982.
762 *Into the Anarchic*, Wick, Pulteney Press, 1985.
763 *Sting*, Blackford, Chapman, 1990. Chapman New Writing series.

ELIZABETH BURNS (1957–)
764 *Ophelia and other poems*, Edinburgh, Polygon, 1991.

PETER DAVIDSON (1957–)
765 *Works in the Inglis Tongue*, Cambridge, Three Tygers Press, 1989.
766 *The Palace of the Sandhaven*, Hackney, The Stourton Press, 1989.

ALAN RIACH (1957–)
767 (With Peter McCarey) *For What It Is*, Christchurch, Untold Books, 1986.
768 *This Folding Map*, Aukland, Aukland University Press, 1990.

ROBERT ALAN JAMIESON (1958–)
769 *Shoormal: A Sequence of Movements*, Edinburgh, Polygon, 1986.

MEG BATEMAN (1959–)
770 *Orain Ghaoil*. Amhráin Ghrá, Dublin, Coiscéim, 1990.
See also *Other Tongues: Young Scottish Poets in English, Scots and Gaelic*, ed. Robert Crawford, St Andrews, Verse, 1990. This anthology prints work by Meg Bateman, W. N. Herbert, David Kinloch and Angela McSeveney.

ROBERT CRAWFORD (1959–)
771 *A Scottish Assembly*, London, Chatto & Windus, 1990.
772 (With W. N. Herbert (1961–)) *Sharawaggi*, Edinburgh, Polygon, 1990.

GRAHAM FULTON (1959–)
773 *Humouring the Iron Bar Man*, Edinburgh, Polygon, 1990.

KATHLEEN JAMIE (1962–)
774 *Black Spiders*, Edinburgh, Salamander Press, 1982.
775 *The Way We Live*, Newcastle-upon-Tyne, Bloodaxe Books, 1987.
See also 744 above.

By listing the young poets above, I have attempted to give a glimpse of what may be in the future. It may be that it will be from the ranks of these young poets, listed above or not, that there will emerge the poets who in the next decade will take Scottish poetry into new territory. These young poets can build on almost a century of revival of Scottish poetry. From that position they could change completely how that revival or renaissance is seen. I have a speculative and optimistic thought; it is of a chronicler a half-century from now introducing a heading to cover an aspect of the period 1990–2040 – a heading that echoes an earlier one in this book – Three Great New Makars.

Index of Poets

General Index